THE
ALPHABET
OF GRACE

OTHER BOOKS BY FREDERICK BUECHNER

FICTION

NONFICTION

THE
ALPHABET
OF GRACE

**FREDERICK
BUECHNER**

HarperSanFrancisco
A Division of HarperCollinsPublishers

These chapters were originally delivered at Harvard University as The William Belden Noble Lectures, 1969.

The poems by Mr. Buechner originally appeared in the *Quarterly Review of Literature*, Fall 1970, Princeton, N.J.

FIkST HarperCollins paperback edition
published in 1989.
LC: 84-48765
ISBN: 0-06-061173-1
ISBN: 0-06-0611790 (pbk.)

93 94 95 CWI 12 11 10 9 8

For my daughter Sharman

TO THE READER

I am a part-time novelist who happens also to be a part-time Christian because part of the time seems to be the most I can manage to live out my faith: Christian part of the time when certain things seem real and important to me and the rest of the time not Christian in any sense that I can believe matters much to Christ or anybody else. Any Christian who is not a hero, Léon Bloy wrote, is a pig, which is a harder way of saying the same thing. From time to time I find a kind of heroism momentarily possible—a seeing, doing, telling of Christly truth—but most of the time I am indistinguishable from the rest of the herd that jostles and snuffles at the great trough of life. Part-time novelist, Christian, pig.

That is who I am. Who you are I do not know, and yet perhaps I know something. I know that like me you wake up each morning to a day that you must somehow live, to a self that you must somehow be, and to a mystery that you cannot fathom if only the mystery of your own life. Thus, strangers though we are, at a certain level there is nothing about either of us that can be entirely irrelevant to the other. Think of these pages as *graffiti* maybe, and where I have scratched up in a public place my longings and loves, my grievances and indecencies, be reminded in private of your own. In that way, at least, we can hold a kind of converse. And there is always some comfort in knowing that Kilroy also was here.

CONTENTS

1 GUTTURALS

(6:45-7:30 a.m.)

At its heart most theology, like most fiction, is essentially autobiography. Aquinas, Calvin, Barth, Tillich, working out their systems in their own ways and in their own language, are all telling us the stories of their lives, and if you press them far enough, even at their most cerebral and forbidding, you find an experience of flesh and blood, a human face smiling or frowning or weeping or covering its eyes before something that happened once. What happened once may be no more than a child falling sick, a thunderstorm, a dream, and yet it made for the face and inside the face a difference which no theology can ever entirely convey or entirely conceal. But for the theologian, it would seem, what happened once, the experience of flesh and blood that may lie at the root of the idea, never appears substantial enough to verify the idea, or at least by his nature the theologian chooses to set forth the idea in another language and to argue for its validity on another basis, and thus between the idea and the experience a great deal intervenes. But there is another class of men —at their best they are poets, at their worst artful dodgers—for whom the idea and the experience, the idea and the image, remain inseparable, and it is somewhere in this class that I belong. That is to say, I cannot talk about God or sin or grace, for example, without at the same time talking about those parts of my own experience where these ideas became compelling and real.

Let me illustrate by quoting a passage from a novel. A young clergyman away from home stretches out in the grass near his father's barn where certain things happen and do not happen.

> He closed his eyes in the warm sunlight . . . and the earth beneath him seemed to tilt this way and that like a great disc. There was the smell of oranges, his arms heavy as stone on the grass. He could hear the buzz of yellow jackets drifting over the compost. Death must come like this. The Reverend Nicolet found behind his father's boardinghouse, no sign of struggle. . . . Only it was not death that was coming,

whatever else. His heart pounded, and he did not dare open his eyes not from fear of what he might see but of what he might not see, so sure now, crazily, that if ever it was going to happen, whatever it was that happened—*joy, Nicolet, joy*—it must happen now in this unlikely place as always in unlikely places: the road to Damascus, Emmaus, Muscadine, stuffy roomful of frightened Jews smelling of fish. Now, he thought, now, no longer daring not to dare, but opening his eyes to, suddenly, the most superbly humdrum stand of neglected trees with somebody's shoe in the high grass and a broken ladder leaning, the dappled rot of last year's leaves.

"Please," he whispered. Still flat on his back, he stretched out his fists as far as they would reach—"Please . . ." then opened them, palms up, and held them there as he watched for something, for the air to cleave, fold back like a tent flap, to let a splendor through. You prayed to the Christ in the people you knew, the living and the dead: what should you do, who should you be? And sometimes they told you. But to pray now this other prayer, not knowing what you were asking, only "Please, please . . ." Somewhere a screen door slammed, and all the leaves were still except for one that fluttered like a bird's wing.

"Please come," he said, then "Jesus," swallowing, half blind with the sun in his eyes as he raised his head to look. The air would part like a curtain, and the splendor would not break or bend anything but only fill the empty places between the trees, the trees and the house, between his hands which he brought together now. "Fear not," he thought. He was not afraid. Nothing was happening except that everything that he could see—the shabby barn, weeds, orchard—had too much the look of nothing happening, a tense, self-conscious innocence—that one startled leaf. He listened for "Feed my sheep . . . feed my lambs . . ." —the old lambs, faces where children lay buried, his children's faces where the old women they would be lay buried: Cornelia, bony and pigeon-breasted at eighty, boring some young divine with memories of "My father . . ." her eyes blurred behind the heavy lenses. "I believe that once by Grandpa's barn he said he saw . . . ."

Two apple branches struck against each other with the limber clack of wood on wood. That was all—a tick-tock rattle of branches—but then a fierce lurch of excitement at what was only daybreak, only the smell of summer coming, only starting back again for home, but oh Jesus, he thought, with a great lump in his throat and a crazy grin, it was an agony of gladness and beauty falling wild and soft like rain. Just clack-clack, but praise him, he thought. Praise him. Maybe all his journeying, he thought, had been only to bring him here to hear two branches hit each other twice like that, to see nothing cross the threshold but to see the threshold, to hear the dry clack-clack of the world's tongue at the approach of the approach of splendor.[1]

Like most theology, most fiction is of course also at its heart autobiography. In the case of this scene I, as the novelist, was being quite direct. In just such a place on just such a day I lay down in the grass with just such wild expectations. Part of what it means to believe in God, at least part of what it means for me, is to believe in the possibility of miracle, and because of a variety of circumstances I had a very strong feeling at that moment that the time was ripe for miracle, my life was ripe for miracle, and the very strength of the feeling itself seemed a kind of vanguard of miracle. Something was going to happen—something extraordinary that I could perhaps even see and hear—and I was so nearly sure of it that in retrospect I am surprised that by the power of auto-suggestion I was unable to make it happen. But the sunshine was too bright, the air too clear, some residual skepticism in myself too sharp to make it possible to imagine ghosts among the apple trees or voices among the yellow jackets, and nothing like what I expected happened at all.

This might easily have been the end of something for me—my faith exposed as superstition which in part I suppose it is, my most extravagant hope exposed as childish which in part I suppose it is—but it was not the end. Because something other than what I expected did happen. Those apple branches knocked against each other, went clack-clack. No more. No less. "The dry clack-clack of the world's tongue at the approach of the approach of splendor." And just this is the substance of what I want to talk about: the clack-clack of my life. The occasional, obscure glimmering through of grace. The muffled presence of the holy. The images, always broken, partial, ambiguous, of Christ. If a vision of Christ, then a vision such as those two stragglers had at Emmaus at suppertime: just the cracking of crust as the loaf came apart in his hands ragged and white before in those most poignant words of all scripture, "He vanished from their sight"—whoever he was, whoever they were. Whoever we are.

Other possible images occur. In the *I Ching*, the sixty-first hexagram represents a gentle wind above and a lake below and is accompanied by this commentary: "The wind blows over the lake and stirs the surface of the water. Thus visible effects of the invisible manifest themselves."

Or I think of breathing—the body in its wisdom taking its sustenance out of the air even when the conscious mind, the will, the hunger both for life and for death, are asleep. I think of the breathing of one who is asleep, how suddenly in some dark passage of the night the breathing becomes a word, the dreamer speaks, and through his word the fragment of a dream passes from inner world to outer world. The visible effects of the invisible manifest themselves.

Or the dream itself, the shadowy acting out against

an inner landscape of some hidden desire, some half-forgotten scrap of the past, some intuition out of the racial memory of mankind like water dipped from a deep well and still tasting of the earth. And then to remember the dream when you wake up, to be transformed a little by what you have learned about who you were or are or might be, is to incarnate the dream, to give hands and feet to a mystery.

Or silence—silence between people, strangers sitting beside each other on a train or at night or taking shelter under the same awning in a rainstorm. Two lives hidden behind faces, divided by fathoms of empty space, wrapped round in silence which one of them breaks then with maybe some word that in one way or another means Know me, Know me, clack-clack, and something that never was before comes into being as the other replies and something is made manifest—a lunar landing, a footprint on an alien star.

Or out of silence prayer happens: waking at night when the silence in your room is no deeper than the silence in yourself because for a moment all thought is stilled and you do not know where you are or possibly even who you are or what you are, and then out of this noplace and nobody that is you, out of this silence that your flesh shells, the prayer comes—O Thou—out of silence, addressed to silence, then returning to silence like the holy syllable OM where it is the silence encircling the sound that is itself most holy.

Or the other way round. All at once or little by little, the disguise of words is dropped, the conversation dwindles like a mist thinning out, and for the first time the shape of another becomes at least partially visible, and eyes meet, or without apology for once hands touch, and the angel who troubles the waters troubles the in-between air and a healing becomes possible. For the miracle at least of the moment the deaf hear and the blind, the blind, see.

You get married, a child is born or not born, in the middle of the night there is a knocking at the door, on the way home through the park you see a man feeding pigeons, all the tests come in negative and the doctor gives you back your life again: incident follows incident helter-skelter leading apparently nowhere, but then once in a while there is the suggestion of purpose, meaning, direction, the suggestion of plot, the suggestion that, however clumsily, your life is trying to tell you something, take you somewhere.

Or random sounds: the clock's tick-tock, voices outside the window, footsteps on the stair, a bird singing, and then just for a moment a hint of melody.

The invisible manifests itself in the visible. I think of the alphabet, of letters literally—A, B, C, D, E, F, G, all twenty-six of them. I think of how poetry, history, the wisdom of the sages and the holiness of the saints, all of this invisible comes down to us dressed out in their visible, alphabetic drab. H and I and J, and K, L, M, N are the mold that our innermost thoughts must be pressed into finally if we are to share them; O, P, Q, R, S, T, U is the wooden tongue that we must speak if we are ever to make ourselves known, that must be spoken to us if we are ever to know. V, W, X, Y, Z. Clack-clack.

I am thinking of incarnation, breath becoming speech through teeth and tongue, spirit becoming word, silence becoming prayer, the holy dream becoming the holy face. I am speaking of the humdrum events of our lives as an alphabet.

I am thinking of grace. I am thinking of the power beyond all power, the power that holds all things in manifestation, and I am thinking of this power as ultimately a Christ-making power, which is to say a power that makes Christs, which is to say a power that works through the drab and hubbub of our lives to make Christs of us before we're done or else, for our sakes, graciously to destroy us. In neither case, needless to say, is the process to be thought of as painless.

I am thinking of salvation. In the movie called *2001, A Space Odyssey,* a man goes hurtling through the universe to the outermost limits of the universe, the outermost limits of space and time. Through huge crevasses of racing light he passes finally beyond space and time altogether, and you sit there in the midnight of the movie theater watching him and wondering what fantastic secret he will discover there at the very secret heart of the fantastic itself, and then comes the movie's most interesting moment. Because when his space pod finally comes to rest, what the man steps out to discover is not some blinding cosmic revelation, some science-fiction marvel, but a room. He steps out into an almost everyday room of floor and ceiling and walls with a table in it and some chairs and a half-filled bookshelf and a vase of flowers and a bed. And in this room the man dies and is born again. At the heart of reality there is a room. At the heart of reality there is a heart beating life into all that lives and dies. Clack-clack.

You wake up out of the huge crevasses of the night and your dreaming. You get out of bed, wash and dress, eat breakfast, say goodbye and go away never maybe to return for all you know, to work, talk, lust, pray, dawdle and do, and at the end of the day, if your luck holds, you come home again, home again. Then night again. Bed. The little death of sleep, sleep of death. Morning, afternoon, evening—the hours of the day, of any day, of your day and my day. The alphabet of grace. If there is a God who speaks anywhere, surely he speaks here: through waking up and working, through going away and coming back again, through people you read and books you meet, through falling asleep in the dark.

If I talk about these things less as lecturer than as storyteller, more anticly than academically, more concretely than conceptually, it is not only because I can do

no other but because it is also the way I believe I have
heard my life talk to me if my life talks to me, the way
even God talks to me if God talks to me. The language
of God seems mostly metaphor. His love is like a red, red
rose. His love is like the old waiter with shingles, the
guitar-playing Buddhist tramp, the raped child and the
one who raped her. There is no image too far-fetched,
no combination of sounds too harsh, no spelling too
irregular, no allusion too obscure or outrageous. The
alphabet of grace is full of gutturals.

"In the beginning God created the heavens and the
earth. The earth was without form and void, and darkness was upon the face of the deep; and the Spirit of
God was moving over the face of the waters. And God
said, 'Let there be light.' " Creation *ex nihilo*. Light out
of darkness; Order out of chaos; Waking out of sleep.
The furnace is turned down and the window open a
crack. The shoes are side by side near the window, their
toes slippery with moonlight and emptiness where flesh
and blood belong. The five-year diary is more than four
years full. Over the mantle Winslow Homer's croquet
players play against a horizon dark as the end of the
world, a man in a straw boater crouching at the feet of a
lady in long skirts to line up her ball. My father's christening mug is half full of water left over from the night
before and tasting of silver. The white wicker rocker
ticks like a clock. The darkness falls on the just and the

unjust, the hero and the pig, the quick, the quicker, and the not so quick. The shoes are my cousins, the table my aunt, the tock of the wicker rocker livelier than my ticker. I do not own these things; we are all things together. I do not have a body; I am a body. And darkness is upon the face of my face.

Beneath the face I am a family plot. All the people I have ever been are buried there—the bouncing boy, his mother's pride; the pimply boy and secret sensualist; the reluctant infantryman; the beholder at dawn through hospital plate-glass of his first-born child. All these selves I was I am no longer, not even the bodies they wore are my body any longer, and although when I try, I can remember scraps and pieces about them, I can no longer remember what it felt like to live inside their skin. Yet they live inside my skin to this day, they are buried in me somewhere, ghosts that certain songs, tastes, smells, sights, tricks of weather can raise, and although I am not the same as they, I am not different either because their having been then is responsible for my being now. I am like a candle lit from a candle lit from a candle, as Gautama said, the traveling flame never the same and never different either. And buried in me too are all the people I have not been yet but might be someday—the Boston Strangler and St. John of the Cross, Heliogabulus and Dagwood Bumstead, Judas Iscariot and Robin Hood and Little Nell, all the lives I have not yet lived like promises not yet kept, dreams waiting for or dreading the possibility of being dreamed.

I am a necropolis. Fathers and mothers, brothers and cousins and uncles, teachers, lovers, friends, all these invisibles manifest themselves in my visibleness. Their voices speak in me, and I catch myself sometimes speaking in their voices. I take a curve at sixty and hear my dead grandfather say, "Take it easy, Buzzfuzz," and I am Buzzfuzz and my grandfather too. Rubbing little circles on the pad of my middle finger with my thumb, I become my grandmother who spoke in paragraphs and wore a black felt tricorne with a black cockade that made her look, she said, ilke *une interrement de la première classe*. Fresh from my second year of Greek, I etymologized *rhododendron* for her once—*rhodos* red and *dendron* tree: red tree—and she said, "That's what you think," looking over my shoulder as I write this to say it again from time to time.

> *Years later, that breakfast burns still like sun*
> *In the bowl of a spoon. Unitarians believe*
> *In at most, you said, one God, and you called him*
> *To witness. "My God!"—with skeins of smoke*
> *From your Chesterfield, the marmalade in flames,*
>   *the star*
> *From your coffee a-swing on the crazy ceiling—*
> *"How I hate these four people."*

Your husband bald as his breakfast egg;
Mounting his muffin the mad dauphin your son;
Your handsome, blue-eyed daughter; and I
Your pimply, rapt idolater.
A joke. We took it so.
Your eyes, buzzard-amber and burning,
Neither hated nor loved but were bored, bored,
My dear dead dear—bored with Carolina sun,
With mountains rising like smoke, with your
    eighty-five years,
But boredom like a coif, a transcendence,
Like Solomon in all his great and tiresome glory.

I am a home movie with endless shots of friends and relations. Old Newpher the Greek teacher chases us around and around the classroom table past a blackboard covered with irregular verbs, and when he catches us, he pinches us hard on the backs of our necks. Long ago I swallowed his blackboard whole, and some of my verbs are still irregular. My skinny first love comes racing through the summer dusk like newspaper caught in the wind, and the Good Humor man tinkles his glockenspiel as we wolf our way down to the possibility of a Lucky Stick. My stick is lucky, and my bony love has a *petit mal* flat on her back on the kitchen linoleum while Sadie, her nurse, tells me it will be over soon, not knowing that in ways she cannot guess, it is not over yet. My luck is sticky.

My tiddly uncle climbed a tree, sat hours
Hairy and black in a forked branch with his smile
Hung crooked, his oystery sneakers jutting like
　　　fungus.
Through the sleeping-porch screen we watched
　　　dampness fall
Until there were pearls in his hair, there were
　　　pearls in his eyes,
And my grandfather pounded the trunk with his
　　　stick: "Come down, sir!
Come down from that tree." My uncle should
　　　never have called him
An old grey rat and swung him around till his
　　　glasses
Fell off on the carpet, should never have climbed
　　　there at all,
I thought, assuming he'd have to come down in
　　　the end
And make everything right. But he never came
　　　down. Summers,
Summers have come and gone, and the old grey
　　　rat
Has been caught in a fool-proof trap, and now
　　　where the sleeping-porch was
There is nothing but sleep. Only my uncle hangs
　　　on.
Strangers no longer can tell him apart from the
　　　tree,
A hairy, black tree shelved all over with fungus,

> *With branches crooked as smiles, and at certain*
> *times,*
> *In certain kinds of rain, as grey as pearls.*

As the reel unwinds further, why the continual re-appearance of the brick house on the left and the steep hill through the bug-flecked windshield? Why the robin with the broken wing dragging across the wet grass?

> *The car I was learning to drive from my mother*
> *bogged down*
> *In the sand at Folly Beach with the tide coming*
> *in,*
> *And a black in persimmon slacks charged ten*
> *dollars to tow.*
> *The horn got stuck, the cash ran low, and the*
> *she-crab soup*
> *Turned out an expensive failure. But all*
> *Was not lost. We had come to see Charleston,*
> *my grandmother, mother,*
> *And I, and we saw it. The old woman who let*
> *down a basket*
> *For breakfast, magnolia and cypress by rainlight,*
> *a grave*
> *Made out of a bedstead, spongy and flaked with*
> *wooden*
> *Pineapple posts that leaned in toward each other.*
> *The bellboy*

Spoke gullah but never found out my secret, not
    even
My grandmother found it out: that I was myself
A bellboy, a boy living under a bell in Charleston
Exhausted with lust and longing, afraid I was
    losing my mind.

Down the three-story stairwell I see my great-grandmother's bald spot. I hold my plush monkey over the bannister and let it drop. Its eyes light up when you squeeze its kidneys as whose eyes, I suppose, would not. Just as it is about to hit the target, the film jumps a sprocket, and on the screen everything goes haywire. I am blinded by the racing crevasses of light.

The old tigers with prostates, the blue-haired
    vamps,
The barber who once lent him money, the child
He swam oceans ago on his shoulders—always
I sought the ones out who remembered my father
The swimmer, the dancer, the charmer of birds
From the trees; sought him under the pictures
In frames, at the bottoms of drawers, a boy
Stretched out on the dunes in a jersey frowning,
Or holding the ball with his year on his chest,
His stick-pin, a letter that started out Blessed.
He went up in a puff of smoke in his thirties
Leaving me in my forties my father's Dutch
    Uncle

To chide him for leaving so soon—before break-
   fast,
Before we were up. In his roadster he waited
Until the exhaust had exhausted him utterly
And not even the uncombed ladies in bathrobes
Could get him back up on his feet.
What I pieced back together never did quite
Do him justice, so I gave up the ghost,
And content myself now with occasional visits
To where he lies many years deep in my over-
   grown face.

The chaos of sleep, the *tohu wabbohu* of dreams. If our waking world, the world of Ten Thousand Things, is threatened by a population explosion, only consider the problem as it exists in the world of dreams where there are not only all the living to domicile but all the dead too not to mention the others, all the might-have-beens and the might-be-yets, the world of Ten Thousand times Ten Thousand Things and un-Things. I dream that I wake up and walk into the living room to find that all the furniture is gone and the walls painted white as a sepulcher. I walk on into the kitchen where in a shower of light I find old Rosa, the German cook, who twenty years ago with her mattress on her back sailed back to Germany to die and died. She jumps as though she has seen a ghost, mark that, and with astonishment asks me what I am doing there for the love of God. It is a curious question and one that I might more reasonably have asked of her since, although I do not choose to press this, it is she after all, is she not, who is the ghost. But the point is that she is there in the kitchen of my dream proving that dreams are inexhaustible and that oneirography transcends geography. There is room for all. The quick and the not so quick and the dead.

Beneath the moonlit drifts of sheet, I turn in my sleep and draw up my knees except that there is no *I* at this moment but just my knees which draw up themselves by some complex autonomy of bones, tendons, muscles, like an empty self-service elevator working off calls from floor to floor after closing time. And with my knees drawn up, I dream I am sitting down. I am sitting on a stool at a bar, and my glass has left a wet ring on the wooden counter-top. With my finger, I start to move the wet around. I move it this way and that way with nothing much on my dream of a mind. And then on the smooth counter of the bar I write a name. When I have finished writing it, I start to weep, and the tears wake me up. I cannot remember the name I wrote, but I know that it was a name that I would be willing to die for. Maybe it was the secret name of God or the secret name of the world. Maybe it was my own secret name. The dream is only a dream, but the tears are exceedingly real.

Darkness was upon the face of the deep, and God said, "Let there be light." Darkness laps at my sleeping face like a tide, and God says, "Let there be Buechner." Why not? Out of the primeval chaos of sleep he calls me to be a life again. Out of the labyrinth of selves, born and unborn, remembered and forgotten, he calls me to be a self again, a single true and whole self. He calls me to be this rather than that; he calls me to be here rather than there; he calls me to be now rather than then. He calls me to be of all things me as this morning when the alarm went off or the children came in or your dream woke you, he called you to be of all things you. To wake up is to be given back your life again. To wake up—and I suspect that you have a choice always, to wake or not to wake—is to be given back the world again and of all possible worlds this world, this earth rich with the bodies of the dead as our dreams are rich with their ghosts, this earth that we have seen hanging in space, our toy, our tomb, our precious jewel, our hope and our despair and our heart's delight. Waking into the new day, we are all of us Adam on the morning of creation, and the world is ours to name. Out of many fragments we are called to put back together a self again.

"My poor misguided child," my grandmother says, "is all this cloudy rhetoric your way of saying that in the morning you wake up?"

"Yes, it is," I say.

"You make it sound like the opening of a three-volume novel," she says, "You make it sound like the opening of *Anna Karenina*, in fact."

"Yes," I say.

"Yes," she says. She is all white linen and wicker and

silver cigarette box and white paper cigarette holder. "Only Tolstoy wasn't so rhetorical," she says.

Prince Oblonsky wakes up, not in his wife's bedroom but on the leather-covered sofa in his study. He turns over his stout, well-cared-for person on the springy sofa as though he would like to sink his face in it. Then all at once he sits up and opens his eyes. He is remembering his dream. It had to do with a dinner in Darmstadt or somewhere, possibly America. There were glass tables, and they were singing "Il mio tesoro" or something better. There were decanters of some sort on the table. There were women. It was all very nice. And then suddenly the Prince remembers that he is not sleeping in his wife's room but in the study. His wife has discovered that he is carrying on with the French governess. Every painful detail of the quarrel comes back as he sits there in his morocco slippers, a birthday present from his wife. And, "What's to be done? What's to be done?" he says to himself in despair.

"There was no solution," Tolstoy writes, "but the universal solution that life gives to all questions, even the most complex and insoluble. That answer is: one must live in the needs of the day—that is forget oneself. To forget himself in sleep was impossible now, at least until night-time; he could not go back now to the music sung by the decanter women; so he must forget himself in the dream of daily life. . . . He put on a grey dressing-gown lined with blue silk, tied the tassels in a knot, and, drawing a deep breath of air into his broad, bare chest, he walked to the window with his usual confident step, turning out his feet that carried his full frame so easily." [2]

"How French that sounds," my grandmother says. "Especially the part about the feet. Can't you just see the old sinner padding across the turkey carpet barefoot while his wife weeps out her heart somewhere? It is like a Frenchman to notice feet at a time like that. It is so unromantic."

The part about the feet is my favorite, that and the part about how it takes him awhile before he remembers who he is. I tell her this.

"The way I understood it," she says, "you were supposed to devote these talks to religious matters. Incarnation and Grace and Salvation were some of the noble words you used."

I say that feet are very religious too. She says that's what you think. I say that if you want to know who you are, if you are more than academically interested in that particular mystery, you could do a lot worse than look to your feet for an answer. Introspection in the long run doesn't get you very far because every time you draw back to look at yourself, you are seeing everything except for the part that drew back, and when you draw back to look at the part that drew back to look at yourself, you see again everything except for what you are really looking for. And so on. Since the possibilities for drawing back seem to be infinite, you are, in your quest to see yourself whole, doomed always to see infinitely less than what there will always remain to see. Thus, when you wake up in the morning, called by God to be a self again, if you want to know who you are, watch your feet. Because where your feet take you, that is who you are.

"Would you mind also running through *rhododendron* again. I want to make sure I have it right," my grandmother says. "Would you consider it crude if I were to say that during my days in the flesh, the first place my feet usually took me was the water closet?"

Oh, but my dear dead dear, what better place? Life is grace. Sleep is forgiveness. The night absolves. Darkness wipes the slate clean, not spotless to be sure, but clean enough for another day's chalking. While he sleeps and dreams, Prince Oblonsky is allowed to forget for a little, to unlive, his unfaithfulness to his wife—his dreaming innocence is no less part of who he is, no less transfiguring and gracious, than his waking adultery—and thus he is cleansed for a little while of his sin, emptied of his guilt. And so are we all. It is fitting that the first place our feet should take us is the water closet. Poor, bare, forked animals that we are, never more truly humble, more cut down to size, more helplessly ourselves than here in the jakes amid the smells of our own mortality, we empty ourselves of the refuse of the day before, we are cleansed of the waste of yesterday. We are no longer now what we were then because in between we have lain insensate in the dark, a cousin to tables and chairs, and dreams have happened, and we have conversed with the dead. We have survived the failures and unfaithfulnesses of yesterday, and life has called us back to life again. It is, within limits, a new life. There is hope for us still.

What is the hope that there is? I see my face in the bathroom mirror. The encounter is unavoidable. Morning after morning it takes place, and morning after morning, year after year, it is the same face that I encounter, neither much better nor much worse for all the times I've washed and shaved it, for all the life I've lived with it and behind it. I have grown accustomed to my face and so have my family and friends. If it does not have in it the power of certain rare faces to rejoice the hearts of all who behold it, under the right circumstances it can moderately rejoice two or three selected faces. It also, as far as I know, causes no one anywhere to be afraid or to despair. I see things in my face that I wish were not there. I see things in my face that I am content to see there. There are times when I see it as almost a stranger's face. But all in all, it is a face that has served me well enough over the years and that I can live with.

What bothers me is simply the everlasting sameness of

my face. Those eyes, that nose, that mouth—the variations of expression they're capable of is really so restricted. The grimmest human tragedy can furrow the brow little more than the momentary pain of the dentist's drill. If an angel of God were to appear suddenly, the eyes that I beheld its glory with could light up little brighter than at the smell of coffee brewing in the morning. More than any other part of me, my face is the part where most of the time I live. It is so hard to disentangle ourselves that I can't be sure whether I am happy and therefore my face smiles or whether my face smiles and therefore I am happy—which is to say that my face and I are so much more involved with each other than my hands and I or my stomach and I that I am forced to conclude that to an alarming degree I *am* my face. Alarming because I am forced to conclude also that the limitations of my face are my limitations, that in more ways than merely spatial, my face is my farthest-flung frontier, the limit beyond which I cannot pass. My alarm as I look in the mirror, toothbrush in hand, is that I can do no more than my face can do, that I can be no better than the face that I have made out of my life and that my life has made out of me.

And yet: O purge me with hyssop and I shall be clean, wash me and I shall be whiter than snow. Out of the depths of my face I cry unto thee that of thy grace, thy mercy and miracle, thou wilt make me more than my face. If thy power is above all the power to make Christs, then reshape this face I wear and am. What hope is there for me? Thou art my only hope.

Prince Oblonsky, newly awake and sitting on the edge of the sofa in his study, asks, "What's to be done?" And the answer that life gives is: live in the needs of the day. What's to be done? Do what you need most to do this day and what is most needed of you. Where your feet take you today is who you are. Guide thou my feet. O Thou invisible, manifest thyself, clack-clack, in this visible day.

Darkness moved upon the face of the something or other, and something like a voice said, "Let there be . . . Buechner. Let there be something like Buechner," and there was, there is, here in the bathroom with sleep in his eyes and the rain washing at the windowpanes as he pulls on his trousers one leg at a time.

Come unto me. Come unto me, you say. All right then, dear my Lord. I will try in my own absurd way. In my own absurd way I will try to come unto you, a project which is in itself by no means unabsurd. Because I do not know the time or place where you are. And if by some glad accident my feet should stumble on it, I do not know that I would know that I had stumbled on it. And even if I did know, I do not know for sure that I would find you there. I do not know for sure that it was indeed your name that made my tears come when I wrote it with my finger in the wet. And if you are there, I do not know that I would recognize you. And if I recognized you, I do not know what that would mean or even what I would like it to mean. I do not even well know who it is you summon, myself.

For who am I? I know only that heel and toe, memory and metatarsal, I am everything that turns, all of a piece, unthinking, at the sound of my name. Am where my feet take me. Buechner. Come unto me, you say. I, Buechner, all of me, unknowing and finally unknowable even to myself, turn. O Lord and lover, I come if I can to you down through the litter of any day, through sleeping and waking and eating and saying goodbye and going away and coming back again. Laboring and laden with endless histories heavy on my back.

2 SIBILANTS

(7:30-8:30 a.m.)

It is an insignificant, humdrum kind of day with no particular agenda, nothing special to do or think or be in it. It is an any-day kind of day with little to distinguish it from either yesterday or tomorrow. You wake up, which is to say you pick up the threads again of your life. For one more day the world is yours. You are your own to name.

In Hindu iconography, the mind of man is portrayed as an ape swinging from tree to tree as the apelike fancy takes him. You smell cooking and, whether you want to or not, think of eating; you pull up the shade to find snow falling, the *snow*, falling, and for a wild second or two are so helplessly God knows what that anything is possible, anything, and the runners of the Snow Queen's sleigh hiss through the enormous drifts; bending over to pick up your watch from the floor by the bed, you know suddenly that you will die someday or that you will never die. Who knows what branch you will leap to next, scratching at your arm-pit with the thumb of the same arm, your tail stiff as a question mark? Who would venture to guess what effect the dream will have upon you which you didn't choose to dream in the first place and can hardly now remember in the second? You are the world's to name. And yet not. The world is yours to name. It is your birthday, and it is you who must give yourself birth, put back together a self again out of all these rags and bobtails. Night has wiped the slate, if not clean as a hound's tooth, at least clean enough. Follow where your feet take you.

You do not so much have a body as you are a body with slapstick needs that must be attended to before you can attend very effectively to anything else, so you attend to them in no more or less slapstick a fashion than William Shakespeare or Miss America or Vice President Agnew or Jesus of Nazareth, all of them padding off to their solitary unburdening, to that earthy and odorous acting out of the grace of life, of God, whereby the dross of the past is continually being abandoned so that each day can be in some measure a new day with its own new set of possibilities, its own new range of resignation and hope. With razor in hand and soap on your chin, you read among other things your doom in your face, the failures, estrangements, betrayals and self-betrayals. And you read mortality in your face—this is the face that you will die with, the face that you will die of. But you read also hope in your face—the hope that by the grace of this new day you may become somehow better than your face. You wash. Because you belong to a race of creatures who hide their nakedness from another, you dress—the lunacy of all those tubes of cloth for arms and legs, those buttons, buckles and flaps. But you are no hero; you dress. And washed, dressed, part hidden, part forgiven, part awake, part named, you are Prince Oblonsky, and the question is, What's to be done? What's to be done.

Forget yourself in the dream of daily life, Tolstoy says, and forget myself, yes. To forget myself in the very process of being myself, I ask no better. Perhaps there is no gift more precious than the gift of spontaneity, the ability of certain men and animals to act straight and fresh and self-forgettingly out of the living center of who they are without the paralyzing intervention of self-awareness. But the dream of daily life, no. I have had enough for awhile of dreams. Certainly it is often dreamlike enough as you move from morning to evening with little sense of how you got from one to the other, as you move from conversation to conversation, living your life like the food you eat in dreams which neither tastes nor nourishes. But I don't want to dream this day out. I want to live this day out. I want to live this day out as though it were the first day of my life because that is of course what it is.

Who knows whether there is life on any other planet anywhere else in the universe, but there is life on this planet. And what is life like? Think of not knowing what life is and then finding out: a book suddenly learning how to read; a rock jutting out into the sea suddenly knowing the thump and splatter of the waves, the taste of salt. You are alive. It needn't have been so. It wasn't so once, and it will not be so forever. But it is so now. And what is it like: to be alive in this maybe one place of all places anywhere where life is? Live a day of it and see. Take any day and be alive in it. Nobody claims that it will be entirely painless, but no matter. It is your birthday, and there are many presents to open. The world is to open.

It rattles softly at the window like the fingers of a child as I sit on the edge of the tub to tie my shoes. It comes down the glass in crooked paths to stir my heart absurdly as it always has, and dear God in Heaven, the sound of it on the roof, on the taut black silk of the umbrella, on the catalpa leaves, dimpling the glassy surface of the peepering pond. It is the rain, and it tastes of silver; it is the rain, and it smells of christening. The rain is falling on the morning of my first day, and everything is wet with it: wet earth, wet fur, the smell of the

grass when it is wet, the smell of the wet pavements of
the city and the sound of tires on the wet streets, the wet
hair and face of a woman doing errands in the rain.
Wherever my feet take me now, it will be to something
wet, something new, that I have never seen before.

You wonder about life on distant worlds if there is
any life on them, the extravagances of nature there, the
convolutions of unimaginable histories and geographies
there, and now on this distant world that is yours and
that you have awakened to, you will see it all for yourself. You have only to look through this rain-washed
glass to see what astronomers from other worlds would
travel light-years to see: this third planet from the sun
with the rain falling, the glint of water taps, tub rim,
through the window the cat licking its silken wrist under
the eaves. The curious rendezvous as you get to your
feet, both shoes tied, and stand there with the whole
weight of you, everything that goes by your name, press-
ing down for all you're worth upon the shaggy pelt of
this planet which with its whole vast bulk and for all its
worth presses up to resist you—this encounter, this tryst,
between you and your planet, each of you so gentle yet
unyielding and firm with the other. And you will see
faces before this first day is done: each the only one of
its kind in the universe, each the face of a high king
whose line reaches back unbroken through unnumbered
generations, through ancient cities and forgotten battles,
past dim, gibbering rain forests to the very beginnings

of history itself and beyond, and they will speak to you in words soft and worn from centuries of handling, will say A, B and C to you, E and F and G and H, and will say O to you, O, O, high king to high king as you meet in the mystery of this rainy morning while the cat buries her mess by the broken red wagon and leaves the color of sunrise fall out of the sky.

A ghost speaks. "My dear lad," she says, "I would give my immortal soul if I were sure I had one for just one taste of that rain on my tongue, one tabby touch of that ramshackle cat. I would give my three-cornered black hat for just the nuisance of X and K again or the lilt and folly of L. And for the sound of my own name on somebody else's lips . . . somebody calling me by name through an open door. . . ." Another life—alive, like you, by the giddy grace of God—reaches across the light-years that separate each from the other and touches your hand and names your name like God the Father on Michelangelo's ceiling who reaches out of the cloud and touches Adam, names Adam's flesh to holy life. On the third planet from the sun you will touch another's life to life and be touched. Be alive this first and holy day because order has been created out of chaos, light out of dark, so you can see, touch, taste, and smell and tell this day that you have never seen before because it has never been before.

"And this day that you will never see again." It is my own ghost this time, the death I will die, who catches me as I step out combed, brushed, shod, into the room where my youngest child lies asleep with a huge snake uncoiled beside her. She lies heavy on her pillows as if she has fallen there, and one arm is around the neck of her temporarily gentle bedfellow. All the days of your life have brought you to this day, the ghost says, and you must live it as though it is your last day as yourself because be assured that it is. You will never see this day again once it has passed, and never again will you be this self.

Plush into scale, tomorrow the snake will curl to strike. You are seeing everything for the last time, and everything you see is gilded with goodbyes. The child's hand like a starfish on the pillow, your hand on the doorknob. Caught between screen and window, a wasp unfolds one wing. With a sick smile, guilt-ridden, the old dachshund lurches off the forbidden couch when you come through the door, his nose dry with sleep, and makes for the pillow by the hot-air register. It is the room where for years Christmases have happened, snow falling so thick by the window that sometimes it has started to snow in the room, brightness falling on tables, books, chairs, the gaudy tree in the corner, a family sitting there snowmen, snowbound, snowblind to the crazy passing of what they think will never pass. And today now everything will pass because it is the last day. For the last time you are seeing this rain fall and in your mind that snow, this child asleep, this cat. For the last time you are hearing this house come alive because you who are part of its life have come alive. All the unkept promises if they are ever to be kept have to be kept today. All the unspoken words if you do not speak them today will never be spoken. The people, the ones you love and the ones who bore you to death, all the life you have in you to live with them, if you do not live it with them today will never be lived.

It is the first day because it has never been before and the last day because it will never be again. Be alive if you can all through this day today of your life. What's to be done? What's to be done?

Follow your feet. Put on the coffee. Start the orange juice, the bacon, the toast. Then go wake up your children and your wife. Think about the work of your hands, the book that of all conceivable things you have chosen to add to the world's pain. Live in the needs of the day.

What's to be done so that I can be better than my face? "Come unto me," I hear, and the words move me more than I can say. Why should they move me? Why shouldn't they leave me cold or bore me to death?

In an elegant house on Long Island one summer Sunday, down a long table cluttered with silver and crystal and the faces and hands of strangers, my hostess suddenly directs a question at me. She is deaf and speaks in the ringing accents of the deaf, and at the sound of her question all other conversation stops, and every face turns to hear my answer. "I understand that you are planning to enter the ministry," she says. "Is this your own idea, or have you been poorly advised?"

I had no answer, and even if I'd had one, it wouldn't have been shoutable, and even if I'd shouted it, she couldn't have heard it, so the question was never answered and thus rings still unanswered in my head. How did I ever get involved in this business to begin with? By what implausible train of circumstances do I find myself standing here now? Why should the words of Jesus move me more than I can say?—Come unto me. Why should I believe in God at all, whatever it means to believe, whatever God means and whatever I mean?

It may all be the melancholy blunder my hostess suggested down the terrible length of her table. Fatherless at ten, I may simply have dreamed some kind of father into some kind of life somewhere else. I have always loved fairy tales and to this day read E. Nesbit and the Oz books, Andrew Lang and the Narnia books and Tolkien with more intensity than I read almost anything else. And I believe in magic or want to. I want flying saucers to be true, and I want life to exist on Mars, and I dream of a heaven where old friends meet and old enemies embrace one another and weep. And just at dawn in an eigheenth-century castle built of rose-colored stone in Dumfriesshire, I have reason to think I saw a ghost. All of which is to say I am a congenital believer, a helpless hungerer after the marvelous as solace and adventure and escape. I am also a fabricator, and

I am willing to believe that the whole business of God in my life may be something I have fabricated out of my need for solace and adventure if not for escape because religion has never seemed escape to me. Escape would be for me to get out of religion—with all its demands and promises—rather than to get into religion. Maybe it is all just a dream. Maybe none of it is true except in some wispy sense true for me. Maybe as that good lady suggested, I was poorly advised to get mixed up with it at all. But I did get mixed up with it, and I am mixed up with it and by it still, and as I stand here in the kitchen waiting for the water to boil, waiting for the time to wake up the children, I must speak of this. Such faith as I have, where did it come from and why?

In my childhood, when you went to the movies in a big city, in between the movies themselves there were often likely to be other entertainments. A curtain would ripple down across the silver screen, for instance, and out of the wall would come silently gliding a vast electric organ with a whole glittering staircase of keyboards and a thousand stops and an organist in a rented tuxedo who would play Ravel's *Bolero* or *Mood Indigo* or the *Ave Maria* from *Faust* with the spotlight on him going blue, green, crimson, and the volume up so high that you could feel it in your teeth. I want to tell you—more crucially, I suppose, I want to tell myself—about such faith as I have and why, but at the same time I have an unnerving vision of myself as the man who used to take the duty at RKO 86th Street—Arlo at the Organ as he was billed on the marquee—swinging out of the wall in his tuxedo as the houselights dim, that corny, nimble-fingered old romancer with his bald spot and his padded shoulders, pulling out all the stops. But I dismiss that vision and ask you to dismiss it. The only accompaniment to these creedal words should be percussive and erratic, a kabuki clatter, the sound of a loose shutter slapping back and forth in the wind, the sound of apple branches knocking against each other clack-clack for no discernible reason and to no discernible end.

I happen to believe in God because here and there over the years certain things happened. No one particularly untoward thing happened, just certain things. To be more accurate, the things that happened never really were quite certain and hence, I suppose, their queer power.

At twenty-seven, living alone in New York trying with no success to start a novel and in love with a girl who was not in love with me, I went to hear a famous preacher preach one morning although I had no idea at the time that he was famous and went only on impulse—I was not a churchgoer—because his church was next door. It was around the time that Elizabeth II was crowned at Westminster Abbey, and the preacher played variations on the theme of coronation. All I remember of what he said is the very last, and that not well, just one phrase of it, in fact, that I'm sure of. He said that Jesus Christ refused a crown when Satan offered it in the wilderness, or something like that. He said that the kingdom of Jesus was not of this world. And yet again and again, he said, Jesus was crowned in the hearts of those who believed in him, crowned king. I remember thinking that was a nice enough image, as images in sermons go, and I remember how the preacher looked up there in the pulpit twitching around a good deal, it seemed to me, and plucking at the lapels of his black gown. And then he went on just a few sentences more.

He said that unlike Elizabeth's coronation in the Abbey, this coronation of Jesus in the believer's heart took place among confession—and I thought, yes, yes, confession—and tears, he said—and I thought tears, yes, perfectly plausible that the coronation of Jesus in the believing heart should take place among confession and tears. And then with his head bobbing up and down so that his glasses glittered, he said in his odd, sandy voice, the voice of an old nurse, that the coronation of Jesus took place among confession and tears and then, as God was and is my witness, *great laughter*, he said. Jesus is crowned among confession and tears and great laughter, and at the phrase *great laughter*, for reasons that I have never satisfactorily understood, the great wall of China crumbled and Atlantis rose up out of the sea, and on Madison Avenue, at 73rd Street, tears leapt from my eyes as though I had been struck across the face.

At twenty-three, I spent two or three days in an Episcopal monastery on the Hudson because I had been told that one of the fathers there was a man who would be able to answer for me some of the more staggering questions that periodically trouble the secret sensualist and would-be believer. When I got there, I discovered that this father I had come to see had gone into retreat and could see nobody—a tendency, I might add, that all my fathers seem to have had in common. I discovered too that all the other fathers and brothers observed what they called the Great Silence so that they couldn't even say good morning when they met you in the corridors but only nodded and smiled as though they knew some joke too rich to tell. Lastly I discovered that the one father whose job it was to speak to visitors was willing to tackle any question I put to him but that a stroke had left his speech so impaired that his words ran together like raindrops on a windowpane and I could understand almost nothing of what he said. So for two or three days I had nothing but silence to listen to—a silence broken mainly, as I remember it, by the sound of rapping on wood strangely enough: the rapping on the door of my cell at daybreak and the muffled cry from the hallway of *Christ is risen;* the abbot rapping on the refectory table to signal the end of our silent meals; the rap-tapping of sandaled feet down the silent corridors. None of the questions that I had come with was answered except as the silence was answer, and the answer of the silence, as I understood it, was that I should myself be silent, which

I was, so silent that after awhile, at least for a time, even my questions were silenced.

I hear the creaking of a chair being tipped back on its hind legs. "Sir, this is all fairly effective in a literary sort of way, I suppose, but since you have already put most of it in a novel, I'm afraid it's a little stale."

My interlocutor is a student who under various names and in various transparent disguises has attended all the religion classes I have ever taught and listened to all my sermons and read every word I've ever written, published and unpublished, including diaries and letters. He is on the thin side, dark, brighter than I am and knows it. He is without either guile or mercy. "You know, you were just getting down to the one thing people might be interested in," he says, "because it is always interesting to hear why a man believes what he believes. But then instead of giving it to them straight, you started paraphrasing from a work of your own fiction. I've heard you do the same sort of thing in sermons. Just as you are about to reach what ought to be the real nub of the matter, you lapse off into something that in the words of one of your early reviewers is either poetry or Williams' Aqua Velva. I would hesitate to use the phrase "artful dodger" if you hadn't already used it artfully yourself. Why don't you really tell them this time? Give it to them straight?"

God. Jesus. The ministry, of all things. Why I believe. He cannot possibly want me to give it straight any more than I want myself to give it straight, get it straight once and for all. For my own sake. I tell him this, and he brushes his hand over his mouth to conceal the glimmer of a smile.

"A question then," he says. "Have you ever had what you yourself consider a genuine, self-authenticating religious experience?"

There are these things I have already mentioned—the monastery visit, the great laughter sermon, the apple tree branches. They all really happened, I tell him, and I don't see why just because I've used them already in a novel I shouldn't use them again now. And the dream of writing the name on the bar. I really dreamed it. God knows I know what he means about artful dodging, but what can be straighter than telling the actual experiences themselves? What more can he want?

"I just told you," he says, "what I want."

Not the least of my problems is that I can hardly even imagine what kind of an experience a genuine, self-authenticating religious experience would be. Without somehow destroying me in the process, how could God reveal himself in a way that would leave no room for doubt? If there were no room for doubt, there would be no room for me.

"I don't think that God would find your case a particular challenge," the interlocutor says. "You have already confessed to a taste for the supernatural. You want to believe in magic and ghosts and flying saucers. If God were to perform just one small miracle, your doubts would fade away like morning dew."

God knows I have prayed for such miracles, both small and great. I confess it. I have prayed for people I knew who were dying of cancer and who went right on with their dying so that if there were healing things that happened this side of healing itself, they were things I could not be sure of except perhaps for the thing inside myself that was healed a little just by praying the prayer. I'm giving it to you straight now, my friend with your chair rocked back and your hands behind your head. Once or twice I thought a true healing happened, but I was not sure, and you are asking for a time I was sure.

I have prayed for some sign, a voice I could hear or a hand I could touch if only for a second in the dark, and here I am a forty-three-year-old American citizen, tax-payer, father of three, who has actually held his hand out in the dark to touch such a hand. And nothing came of it that I could be sure of, no unquestionable sign, unless perhaps the sign of my own hand reaching out with a longing I cannot question.

Driving home from church one morning full of Christ, I thought, giddy in the head almost and if not speaking in tongues at least singing in tongues some kind of witless, wordless psalm, I turned on the radio for the twelve o'clock news and heard how a four year old had died that morning somewhere. The child had kept his parents awake all night with his crying and carrying on, and the parents to punish him filled the tub with scalding water and put him in. These parents filled the scalding water with their child to punish him and, scalding and scalded, he died crying out in tongues as I heard it reported on the radio on my way back from of all places church and prayed to almighty God to kick to pieces such a world or to kick to pieces Himself and His Son and His Holy Ghost world without end standing there by the side of that screaming tub and doing nothing while with his scrawny little buttocks bare, the hopeless little four-year-old whistle, the child was lowered in his mother's arms. I am acquainted with the reasons that theologians give and that I have given myself for why God does not, in the name of human freedom must not, by the very nature of things as he has himself established that nature cannot and will not, interfere in these sordid matters, but I prayed nonetheless for his interference.

"You were going to explain why you believe," the interlocutor says, not unkindly.

I believe without the miracles I have prayed for then; that is what I am explaining. I believe because certain uncertain things have happened, dim half-miracles, sermons and silences and what not. Perhaps it is my believing itself that is the miracle I believe by. Perhaps it is the miracle of my own life: that I, who might so easily not have been, am; who might so easily at any moment, even now, give the whole thing up, nonetheless by God's grace do not give it up and am not given up by it. There is maybe no such thing, old friend and adversary, as a genuine, self-authenticating experience of anything, let alone God. Maybe at the latter day my redeemer shall stand upon the earth and mine eyes shall behold him and not as a stranger, but in the meantime I behold him on the earth as a name which when I write it wakes me up weeping, as a joke too rich to tell on certain silent faces, occasionally even my own face; as a hand which I am able sometimes to believe that only the thin glove of night I wear keeps me from touching.

The alphabet of grace is full of sibilants—sounds that can't be shouted but only whispered: the sounds of bumblebees and wind and lovers in the dark, of white-caps hissing up flat over the glittering sand and cars on wet roads, of crowds hushed in vast and vaulted places, the sound of your own breathing. I believe that in sibilants life is trying to tell us something. The trees, ghosts, dreams, faces, the waking up and eating and working of life, are trying to tell us something, to take us some-where. If this is above all a Christ-making universe, then the place where we are being taken is the place where the silk purse is finally made out of the sow's ear, and the word that life is trying to speak to us is that little by little, squealing and snuffling all the way, a pig either starts turning into at least the first primal, porcine version of a hero, or else is put out of his piggish misery. At the heart of reality—who would have guessed it?—there is a room for dying and being born again.

How do I happen to believe in God? I will give one more answer which can be stated briefly. Writing novels, I got into the habit of looking for plots. After awhile, I began to suspect that my own life had a plot. And after awhile more, I began to suspect that life itself has a plot.

My dark friend has withdrawn to where, like the Cheshire Cat, nothing is left of him but a smile that hovers uncertainly somewhere between my nose and my chin.

The coffee and toast are made, the frozen orange juice unfrozen. The rain is slanting down past the kitchen window, and out in the pasture the horses stand with their backs to it. The clock on the wall is ten minutes fast. I have ten minutes more to live than the clock acknowledges; ten minutes more, as the saying goes, of grace. It is time to wake up the children.

I start with the two older ones because they have to get off to school. Sometimes they only pretend to be asleep, but this time they are not pretending. The shades are drawn, and it is dark in their room so I raise a shade to let the rainlight in.

On the day that he made the earth and the heavens, when no plant of the field had yet sprung up and a mist went up from the earth and watered the whole face of the ground, then the Lord God formed man of dust from the ground and breathed into his nostrils the breath of life, and man became a living being. . . . The older

one lies there skinny and flushed with one arm crooked
at an odd angle over her head. The younger one is curled
up on her side with her face half buried in pillow. I hate
to wake them up for some reason, I'm not sure why. Because sleep is money in the bank, I suppose, and they're
so peaceful there asleep and still with the small rain raining down. I hate to wake them up because sleep is good
for them, which is maybe another way of saying I hate
to wake them up because life is bad for them, only I
don't believe that really. And yet the thought crosses
my mind under its own steam as for all I know it crossed
the mind of God as he stood there shaping the dust in
his hands that was maybe about to be Adam. Buried
somewhere in their faces lie the faces of the old women
that life will make of them someday: Katherine angular
and shrill at eighty; Dinah fat and widowed, boring the
bridge table at a resort hotel with how her father put
her in a lecture once. Who did you say your father was,
my dear?

Life will be bad for them someday, needless to say,
bad for us all before we're done, but I wake them up
anyway into this rainy morning because it is not good
for man to be alone and I need them more than they
or I know to be whoever I am. I suppose that if the
occasion presented itself, I would even die for them
—not heroically like the dinner-jacketed millionaires
on the *Titanic* helping their ladies into the last lifeboats,

but just piggishly as usual, because I couldn't help myself.

I am Adam, and it is my birthday, and the world is mine to name, and *Katherine*, I say, and the whole creation stops breathing or starts breathing as I reach out to touch the sleeping hand. All flesh is grass and like the flower of the field fades, and yet the morning stars sing together and all the sons of God shout for joy as she raises her head and opens one eye the color of wet slate. Two is not twice one, G. K. Chesterton wrote. Two is a thousand times one. For all I know maybe it was not even good for God to be alone.

Creation is underway. Breakfast is underway. Steam from the tea kettle is fogging up the windows. The cat mews to be let in out of the wet. Getting her bathrobe hooked on the knob of a drawer as she tears by, my wife throws up her hands: "Is it going to be *this* kind of a day?" With my ear to the radio, I try to catch what the weather will be. Somebody is crying while somebody else says it is her own fault that she is crying. We break fast together, break bread together fast, with the clock on the wall over my wife's head tick-tocking our time away, time away. Soon it will be time to leave for school. Soon enough it will be time to leave.

At Emmaus, that queer, sad, scared time, it was just after the bread was broken that Jesus vanished from their sight, and when the bread is broken maybe everything always vanishes except the bread itself. B is for bread and for butter both, C is for coffee and cream. D is for I don't know what, but E is for eggs and F is for filling and forgetting and finding as in filling yourself full here —butter and bread and coffee and eggs—you forget yourself here in the crescendo and crumbs of it, and in forgetting yourself find yourself, are yourself. All those Zen storics about some deadhead going to some Zen master and saying one way or another, "Learned one, help me to understand myself," and the learned one saying one way or another, "Produce this self, and then I will help you to understand it," and the dead-head saying, "But surely a self is not something that can be produced," and the learned one saying, "Now at last you understand," and probably letting him have it in the eye with his trick boutonnière for good measure.

You do not have a self, you are a self, and here at breakfast this becomes true. You do not look at yourself in any mirror here and judge yourself, question yourself, fear and hope and pray for yourself. You forget yourself in filling your face. Your hunger for B-is-for-butter-and-bread is your hunger to be alive, and you forget and find yourself both in filling your face here with life. Maybe the reason Jesus vanished from the sight of those two bewildered Jews was that once the bread was broken, their mouths were full of life even without him. For the moment at least he could afford to vanish.

Here with butter on my chin and egg on my tie,

I forget myself in the recitative of my children, the arias of myself and my wife, the patter songs and yammering quintets. It need not always happen that way in a family, but this morning we are lucky, all of us caught up together in the comic opera of being at breakfast and being with each other and being ourselves and alive. We are noisy and talk with our mouths full. We are far from always considerate of each other. Some of us cry, and some of us thump the table for a little silence, a little respect. But instead of standing each in the wings of his own face awaiting the cue to enter and sing some bravura passage, we are caught up together in a common cacophony. Here at this table by rainlight we manage somehow to escape our faces and meet on that common ground where miracles have been known to happen, often the same most ancient and holy miracle.

With varying degrees of misgiving, my wife and I several years ago joined what was called in those days a group-dynamics group and met with a number of other couples in a basement room in New Hampshire for what was only a month or two but seemed a whole long and painful adolescence. The structure was of course that there should be no structure, no set topic to pursue and no set aim to accomplish. The psychiatrist in our midst sat most of the time in a poker-faced, therapeutic silence, and sometimes we would all sit in silence avoiding each other's eyes or any giveaway slouch or jostle or change of seat. But sometimes the conversation worked, and then a kind of invisible spotlight would appear and go moving around among us, stopping for a moment on this one and that one and then on to another one until finally it would come to rest on some particular one and stay there. And this one would then become the center of the group's attention. He would be given the chance to sing his song and tell his tale, and questions would be asked and judgments would be made. For days I found myself both hoping for and dreading the moment when I would be spotted myself as finally I was.

The spotlight fell upon me, the air of the room full of promise and threat, and then suddenly another member of the group, one of the women, did something or other. Perhaps she started to weep, or she laid her head on somebody's shoulder or just got up to change her seat, but the effect was of course to wrest the spotlight from me, to take my moment away before it had a chance to happen, before I had a chance to happen, and then before I knew it, I found myself blurting out what was probably the only authentic utterance I'd managed there yet. It had been my moment, my time, I told her, and now it was her moment, and I hoped she was satisfied, or something like that. And then the ancient and I suppose holy thing happened, the miracle, if you're given to such terms.

A man spoke who was a teaching colleague of mine

and also, I suspected, because he was on the thin side, dark, brighter than I was, my interlocutor in one of his more effective disguises. What he said was, "That's all right, Freddy. Don't be upset. We love you too." *We love you*, he said, of all inane and shattering things he could have said, and he meant it, I could tell, that most unsentimental man in that most unlikely of places.

Whatever "we love you" means, he meant—that at least for a moment they had seen who I was, really saw more or less who it was who had been sitting there in that face all those weeks awaiting and dreading his time, and they wished me well, they willed my good, my peace. It was only then that I realized that this was why I had kept coming all those weeks and why perhaps they had all of them kept coming, perhaps even in some sense why I have come here to speak to you now and why you have come to listen: to be known, to be forgiven, to be healed, which I suppose is to say, if the word is not beyond all hope of salvage, to be loved. This ancient and most holy miracle.

God knows it does not happen often, not even at breakfast time among people who might possibly be willing to die for each other if the chips were down, and often it happens least where it is most needed. A tanned, soft-spoken man has something wrong with his blood which is not at all soft-spokenly killing him. He is my friend, and when he was not dying, I always sought him out especially to be with, but now I go to see him only because I am—was it your own idea, or were you poorly advised?—a priest of sorts, and if the interlocutor, that prosecuting attorney, should press me for another reason for believing in God, I would say that I believe in him because it is only by the grace of something like God that I can do something as much braver than my face as visiting this good man whose pain makes awkward strangers of us. But if grace gets me there, it gets me no further. We cannot make ourselves known to each other; we are not healed and forgiven by each other's presence. With words as valueless as poker chips, we play games whose object it is to keep us from seeing each other's cards. Chit-chat games in which "How are you?" means "Don't tell me who you are," and "I'm alone and scared" becomes "Fine thanks." Games where the players create the illusion of being in the same room but where the reality of it is that each is alone inside a skin in that room, like bathyspheres at the bottom of the sea. Blind man's buff games where everyone is blind.

It is no wonder that we have had to invent other games to counteract these. Encounter groups, T groups, the multisensory techniques of William Schutz and the Esalen Institute and the Living Theater. After all these years of playing games whose purpose it is to keep us at arm's length from one another, to hide from each other our nakedness and our humanity, we turn at last to games no less pathetic and foolish in their ways but whose purpose is nonetheless to help us meet without disguise, to touch without embarrassment, to be human without fear. The sacrament of the Lord's Supper was such a game, I imagine, was once such a supper, such a breakfast, with bread being broken, people praying with their mouths full, and the priest thumping the table for a little silence, all of them caught up in some hallowed middle ground where God knows what was celebrated—the breadness of bread, the transfiguring miracle of bread shared, the passing of a common cup from lip to lip and tipsy kiss of peace, breath laden with bread, wine, miracle.

"As a Unitarian," my grandmother says, "I never went in much for miracles," closing the yellow-backed French novel down over one finger to keep her place. "What is a miracle, dear boy?"

"I still miss you sometimes," I say. "I miss your black three-cornered hat. I miss your letters. I miss your salad dressing. I'm sorry you didn't hang on long enough for my children to know you."

"You brought the oldest one to see me once in that wretched nursing home," she says, "and in place of the grandmother of legend, she saw an old crone propped up in bed over a Double-Crostic. You've had an expensive education. Tell me, what is a miracle?"

"*Rhodos*-red, *dendron*-tree. Rhododendron," I say. It is still raining outside, and the clock is ten minutes fast. The youngest child has dropped her bacon into her milk, and "I knew what kind of a day it was going to be," my wife says, "the minute I caught my sleeve on that damned knob."

A miracle is when the whole is greater than the sum of its parts. A miracle is where one plus one equals a thousand.

Maybe it is a miracle that happens when you shake hands with your left hand instead of your right hand. A student I had known stepped unexpectedly out of a blizzard one evening before supper and at half our average age seemed eerily older than any of us as he told us about his summer with a group on an island somewhere that experimented with the Esalen kind of games. I asked if there were any we could play there in that room with the snow coming down outside, that island, and he started us off by having us all stand up and shake hands—my wife and I and another couple and that slightly miraculous boy all moving around through the firelight and with varying degrees of inhibition each shaking hands with the others not by the right hand but by the left hand. Right hand, left hand, what difference should it make except of course that it makes all the difference because right hands have long since forgotten how to clasp in any but a chit-chat way, and right hands touching do not often touch life into each other as on Michelangelo's ceiling they do, Adam there and the old man in the cloud reaching out to each other. But the left hand has the advantage of inexperience.

The left hand is the country-cousin gawking down Broadway, and to clasp left-handed is for a moment at least to clasp of all things another human hand, and one plus one is more than two.

The boy worked us through other games until finally the hardest of all which was not speaking for fifteen minutes and communicating if at all without words. The other wife picked a photograph album out of the bookshelf and started leafing through the pictures there of other places, other times, other people. At which point the somewhat miraculous boy who had swelled our ranks from four to something rather more than five took a camera out of the knapsack that he'd brought with him through the snowstorm and snapped a picture of her with those pictures in her lap. At the click of the shutter, her head snapped up, and in my mind I can still see the expression on her firelit face as she raised it like a question to him. There was astonishment in her face and irritation and embarrassment and a cry for some kind of mercy and, more than anything else, a bewildered and bewildering beauty. And she stuck out her tongue at him, a marvel and mystery. "Here and now," the boy said later, "she was psyching out, looking at those pictures. I was trying to tell her she was part of a picture herself. She was part of these people and this place. She belonged to this time."

Here and now. This day is our last day and our first day and our only day, and if it's necessary to play idiotic games to make it seem so, if it's necessary to play idiotic games to make it possible to be idiotic and human together, than it is worth playing them. I belong to this breakfast time, and the ten minutes grace was only ten minutes and is over and done. It is time to put on raincoats that smell of childhood and to say goodbye and to drop the children off at school and say goodbye, goodbye, and go off to what it embarrasses me to call my work because it is my idiotic game instead, my solitaire, played out in an empty room where when I'm lucky, I manage to escape everything including the question whether there is anything anywhere that the world needs less in its pain than another lecture, another sermon, another book.

Goodbye. Goodbye. Leaning down with my hand on her shoulder, my face touches my wife's face, coffee on our breaths, and glancing back at her from the door, I am for an instant aware of how the air between us flattens out a little, bows, like a hayfield when the breeze comes up. Marriage becomes right hands clasped. But sometimes goodbye breaks them apart just long enough for them to clasp again, left-handed.

On jeep wheels we roll down the wet mountain, the children and I, with rain on the canvas roof and the wipers slap-slapping, a tent, a world. The hills have begun to turn rusty with fall. All journeys are one journey. One October we left the front door open for the leaves to come through, and for most of a week they sifted in, gold and brown, over the hall carpet until we finally swept them out again and closed the door. You can handle only so much life in a house, only so much death. When we reach the valley, the fog is so thick I turn the headlights on. I ask the youngest one what she wants to be when she grows up, and she says she wants to be green. Why not? We pass the time in the fog playing Ghosts. *To* becomes *tom* becomes *tomorrow*, ending on Dinah. She adds an R to H,E,A, planning on *heart* but *hear* happens first to her grief, and finally *skiing* is the end of her. With the double I and N there is nowhere else to go, and she becomes three thirds of a ghost and we can no longer talk to her because in the profundity of the game to talk to a ghost is to become a ghost yourself. Yet not to talk to her proves ghostlier still. We agree to forget the game.

When the time comes to say goodbye, they are too busy dropping their books and remembering about the sneakers that they forgot to bring for gym to say it, chattering like magpies in their green rubber hoods until in the crowd at the open double doors I can no longer tell which of these lives are my life. When Mark Twain's second child, Susy, died, he said that her death was like a man's house burning down—it would take years and years to discover all that he had lost in the fire . . . all that I lose watching the double doors swallow them up, a foolish, middle-aged man mooning after his children in the rain when there is a whole world crying out in tongues.

Driving on to work alone I think of Mark Twain toward the end of his days riddled with guilt and fame, resplendent in his white suit, people rising to their feet and applauding him when he so much as entered a restaurant.

"Well sir," Captain Stormfield says when he appears before Saint Peter and has difficulty explaining where he's from. "I don't seem to make out which world it is I'm from. But you may know it from this—it's the one the Savior saved."

The head clerk bends his head at the name. Then he says, "The worlds he has saved are like to the gates of heaven in number—none can count them." [3]

But Clemens was never able to swallow it himself, the old prima donna, for all his wife's having badgered him to until finally she lost her own faith and he felt guilty about that too and probably was. Man is like a cholera germ in the blood stream of a tramp named Blitzowski, he wrote in his old age, and Blitzowski is a thief, his body a sewer, a rack of decay, and he is our world, our globe, the lord of our universe. Which was the dream, the grim old comedian finally asked—were his awful dreams dreams or was life itself a dream more awful still? "There is no God," he wrote, "no universe, no human race, no earthly life, no heaven, no hell. It is all a dream—a grotesque, foolish dream. Nothing exists but you. And you are but a *thought*—a vagrant thought, a useless thought, a homeless thought, wandering forlorn among the empty eternities." [4]

And then there is a strange, wild novel which few people I've asked have ever read, *The Man Who Was Thursday*,[5] subtitled *A Nightmare*, in which G. K. Chesterton, the author, confronts the same emptiness in a series of surrealist images which have haunted me since I first read the book as a child. He writes about a group of anarchists whose purpose is not merely to abolish a few despotisms and police regulations but in the long run to abolish God himself. The central council of the anarchists is composed of seven men, each named for a day of the week, and their President is a huge enigma of a man named Sunday. His enormous plans were too obvious to be detected, Chesterton wrote, his enormous face like the mask of Memnon in the British Museum, too frank to be understood, his jokes so big and simple that no one had thought of them as he sat like a great balloon on a balcony overlooking Leicester Square plotting the overthrow of the world. The post of Thursday falls vacant, and the man elected to fill it is secretly a policeman sworn to uphold, of course, the very forces of law and order which the anarchists are dedicated to destroying.

The greater part of the novel consists of a series of marvelous, lunatic chapters in which Thursday discovers

one by one that the five other unbelievably sinister-look-
ing members of the Central Council are all policemen in
disguise like him, and when they compare notes, they
discover that all of them, like Thursday, became policemen in the same way. They were all commissioned by a
chief they never saw because he received them in a
pitch-dark room. Finally, with terror in their hearts,
they confront Sunday with the truth about themselves
and demand that he tell them at last the truth about
himself.

"I? What am I?" roared the President, and he rose
slowly to an incredible height, like some enormous
wave about to arch above them and break. . . .
"You will understand the sea, and I shall still be a rid-
dle; you shall know who the stars are, and not know
who I am. Since the beginnings of the world all men
have hunted me like a wolf—kings and sages, and
poets and law-givers, all the churches, and all the philosophies. But I have never been caught yet, and the
skies will fall in the time I turn to bay. I have given
them a good run for their money, and I will now."

And then before any of them could move:

The monstrous man had swung himself out like
some huge ourang-outang over the balustrade of the
balcony. Yet before he dropped, he pulled himself up

again as on a horizontal bar and thrusting his great chin over the edge of the balcony said solemnly, "There's one thing I'll tell you though about who I am. I am the man in the dark room, who made you all policemen."

Later, after a bizarre chase through London, they come upon Sunday once more "draped plainly in a pure and terrible white," his hair "like a silver flame upon his forehead." The six policemen are gathered about him, each dressed in a robe embroidered with the creatures created on his day of the week, and Sunday addresses them again.

"Let us remain together a little, we who have loved each other so sadly, and have fought so long. I seem to remember only centuries of heroic war, in which you were always heroes—epic on epic, iliad on iliad, and you always brothers in arms. Whether it was but recently (for time is nothing), or at the beginning of the world, I sent you out to war. I sat in the darkness, where there is not any created thing, and to you I was only a voice commanding valour and an unnatural virtue. You heard the voice in the dark, and you never heard it again. The sun in heaven denied it, all human wisdom denied it. And when I met you in the daylight I denied it myself. . . . But you were men. You did not forget your secret honor, though the whole cosmos turned an engine of torture to tear it out of you. I knew how near you were to hell. . . ." There was complete silence in the starlit garden, and then the black-browed Secretary, implacable, turned in his chair towards Sunday, and said in a harsh voice, "Who and what are you?"

"I am the Sabbath," said the other without moving. "I am the peace of God."

The windshield wipers slap back and forth, and the rain rattles on the roof. Come unto me whoever you are and to whoever I am through whatever terrors the dark holds for you. Most of the shops aren't open yet. As I drive by, I recognize the manager of the supermarket smoking a cigar under his umbrella to open up that Uffizi, that Louvre, which he runs from behind dimpled glass up to his chin, watching out over the glittering corridors where ladies in trances follow pushcarts past tiers of shelves too marvelous to name. He must lose himself in his managing as even now the children must be losing themselves in the paint-box colored rooms where with safety scissors and library paste they learn to snip out in heart shapes and pumpkin shapes the tragic history of their race; as my wife must be losing herself in the business now of dishes, beds, washers and dryers and dust. I envy all those whose labors lie outside their skins.

The windshield wipers, the rat-tat of my feet on the

wet pavement, the rattle of the winch as across the street the Ben Franklin man cranks down his awning.

. . . A rung of the broken ladder lay near Nicolet's hand, and he picked it up. "I want you to listen to something. Just sit right where you are." . . .

Denbigh hooked his glasses back over his ears and craned around to see what Nicolet was doing. Nicolet took the ladder rung and gave one of the branches two sharp raps. . . .

"Could you dance to that?" he asked.

"Dance?" Denbigh raised one hand, the fingers spread apart, and touched his brow with it, staring at Nicolet through the fingers—a small, intelligent animal peering out of his cage of flesh.

"If the life of faith was a dance, Denbigh, and this was the only music—all you could hear anyway—" with a few more double taps he began to suggest a kind of erratic rhythm, "—do you think a man could dance to it, Denbigh?"

"It sounds like calypso or something. I suppose you could dance to it," Denbigh said. "I'm not sure what you're talking about."

"I'm not sure what I'm talking about either." He tossed the rung toward the barn where it struck and fell. "But whatever this is we move around through . . ." He raked his hand slowly back and forth through the air. "Reality . . . the air we breathe

. . . this emptiness. . . . If you could get hold of it by the corner somewhere, just slip your fingernail underneath and peel it back enough to find out what's there behind it, I think you'd be—"

Roy had appeared on the back porch and cupping his mouth with one hand, called to them through the still morning haze. "Breakfast," he called. "Breakfast." His shoulders hunched, he leaned forward over the railing.

"I think the dance that must go on back there," Nicolet began, "way down deep at the heart of space, where being comes from. . . . There's dancing there, Denbigh. My kids have dreamed it. Emptiness is dancing there. The angels are dancing. And their feet scatter new worlds like dust." He raised one arm to show his father that he had heard him, but he did not turn. Some magic in his voice had lulled Denbigh, the frown had gone. He sat there listening as though he could hear the angels himself, the lenses of his glasses afire with the splendor of their wings. "If we saw any more of that dance than we do, it would kill us sure," Nicolet said. "The glory of it. Clack-clack is all a man can bear." [6]

3 ABSENCE OF VOWELS
(8:30 a.m.-11 p.m.)

In the parish house of a church, I work in a room which on Sundays is used for Sunday school. The window by the table where I work has large, old-fashioned panes with wavy places and blisters in the glass so that when the sun shines through, it makes Andrew Wyeths on the broad window sill where the white paint is flaking off. Each morning I approach this room as Prince Oblonsky must have approached the French governess who was his mistress: with a mixture of dread and desire. There is a child-sized conference table with ten kindergarten chairs around it. There is a blackboard with two singularly angry trees drawn on

73

it in chalk. Each tree has three branches sticking almost straight up in the air, and at the end of each branch are three desperate fingers. On the ground there is some kind of creature which seems to have a moustache—perhaps a walrus. At the top of the picture, just beneath a stormy mat of blue-chalk sky, the title of the picture is written—*Jesus Answers a Question*—and beneath it a name that I assume to be the artist's: Jane McWilliams. What is the question that Jesus answered? Why are the trees so angry, and what is the creature with the walrus moustache doing there? What am I doing here in this room myself, coming here day after day?

At its heart, I think, religion is mystical. Moses with his flocks in Midian, Buddha under the Bo tree, Jesus up to his knees in the waters of Jordan: each of them responds to something for which words like *shalom*, oneness, God even, are only pallid, alphabetic souvenirs. "I have seen things," Aquinas told a friend, "that make all my writings seem like straw." Religion as institution, as ethics, as dogma, as social action—all of this comes later and in the long run maybe counts for less. Religions start, as Frost said poems do, with a lump in the throat, to put it mildly, or with the bush going up in flames, the rain of flowers, the dove coming down out of the sky.

As for the man in the street, any street, wherever his own religion is a matter of more than custom, it is likely to be because, however dimly, a doorway opened in the air once to him too, a word was spoken, and, however shakily, he responded. The debris of his life continues to accumulate, the Vesuvius of the years scatters its ashes deep and much gets buried alive, but even under many layers the tell-tale heart can go on beating still. Where it beats strong, there starts pulsing out from it a kind of life that is marked by, above all things perhaps, compassion: that sometimes fatal capacity for feeling what it is like to live inside another's skin and for knowing that there can never really be peace and joy for any until there is peace and joy finally for all. Where it stops beating altogether, little is left religiously speaking but a good man, not perhaps in Mark Twain's "the worst sense of the word" but surely in the grayest and saddest: the good man whose goodness has become cheerless and finicky, a technique for working off his own guilts, a gift with no love in it which neither deceives nor benefits any for long.

Religion as a word points essentially, I think, to that area of human experience where in one way or another man happens upon mystery as a summons to pilgrimage, a come-all-ye; where he is led to suspect the reality of splendors that he cannot name; where he senses meanings no less overwhelming because they can only be hinted at in myths and rituals, in foolish, left-handed games and cloudy novels; where in great laughter perhaps and certain silences he glimpses a destination that he can never know fully until he reaches it. To the many

in the world who wistfully or scornfully would deny
ever having had such an experience, the answer, I suspect, is that we are all of us more mystics than we believe
or choose to believe—life is complicated enough as it is,
after all, and I don't want to know why the trees are
angry. We have seen more than we let on, even to ourselves. Through some moment of beauty or pain, some
sudden turning of our lives, through some horror of the
twelve o'clock news, some dream, some breakfast on
the first and last of all our days, we catch glimmers at
least of what the saints are blinded by. Only then, unlike
the saints, more pigs always than heroes, we tend to go
on as though nothing has happened. To go on as though
something *has* happened even though we are not sure
what it was or just where we are supposed to go with it,
is to enter that dimension of life that religion is a word
for.

Some, of course, go to the typewriter. First the lump
in the throat, the child's eye opening like a flower, the
rain on the roof, and then the clatter of A, B, C, D, E,
F, G, the ting-a-ling of the right-hand margin. One
thinks of Pascal sewing into his jacket where after his
death a servant found it his "since about half-past ten
in the evening until about half-past midnight, FIRE.
Certitude. Certitude. Feeling. Joy. Peace," stammering
it out like a child because he had to. *Fire, fire,* and then
the scratch of pen on paper. There are always some who
have to set it down in black and white.

An old friend of mine who has seen immeasurably more of fire than I have seen and who more than anyone else at a crucial time made prayer seem crucial and real to me although I am still very bad at praying, told me how she starts her day in a room not unlike this one where I work. She sits in silence for awhile, trying, without trying too hard, to be silent inside and empty and open, and then, she says, she prays: "I sign myself with the sign of the cross," which she does then with her hand, a large cross from forehead to navel and from shoulder to shoulder; then she prays: "I cover myself with the blood of the lamb"—"I usually don't like that blood-of-the-lamb talk overly much," she said, "but I use it here anyway;" then she prays: "I circle myself with the light of the cross," and sometimes, she says, she will stand up at this point, as she did when she told me about it, and with one hand above her head will draw a circle around her once, as she also did when she told me about it—a small female person standing up with her eyes closed and drawing a magic circle around herself once in the air. Then she says, "In the name of Jesus Christ," and significantly perhaps I can't remember what it is exactly that in the name of Jesus Christ she bids happen or not happen. But sitting at my table in the room where Jane McWilliams did her picture, I speak the formula as she taught it to me, not as an act of piety so much as an incantation of longing.

It is magic, of course, but no matter. I have always

wanted to believe in magic, and it is white magic, certainly, a good spell as spells go and cast only on myself. And this morning, sitting down at the table where I work, I cast it again as Agnes taught me. "I sign myself with the sign of the cross," I pray: that gallows, that rack, that pendant glittering between the breasts of girls and rattling at the hairy pectorals of saints and frauds. "I cover myself with the blood of the lamb," I pray: dark from the jugular of the beast slain in its innocence on an altar smelling of rancid fat, blood the scarlet of martyrs and cardinals, their hats and gloves and little pointed shoes, the wailing Jesus hymns and sinners' scouring. "I circle myself with the light of the cross," I pray: he said, "Let there be," and there was, of course, light, the light that gave me back the world again this morning, that filtered amber and indigo down on old Arlo at his 86th Street organ, the light in the eyes of the green Roman berets who watched another Jew cash in and in the eyes of the Jew, and the light in the room where they let the water run till it was hot enough.

"In the name of Jesus Christ," I pray, and then what? "Let me fall into no sin this day nor run into any kind of danger," I pray. The Lord Jesus Christ and the power of his name. Jesus. The power of any name, spoken, clack-clack, at the fullness of time to break your heart or rejoice your heart. Both maybe. All the invisibleness of a life made manifest in the visible name. My father's name where to say goodbye he wrote it in pencil on the last page of the last book, *Gone with the Wind*, that he read, and all the mystery in this signature of his wandering from job to job after the apotheosis of college, his astonishment at discovering, he who had been a guest all his life and life his host, that when troubles forced him home, he of all people had nowhere to go home to. The name of a friend coming up in the conversation of a stranger so that the friend is suddenly there in the stranger's face. The name of someone you once were in love with. The name that in certain places, at certain times, it would be unbearable to name. The name that can open doors or drop jaws. The names of places: Auschwitz and Roncevalles, Hamburg Hill, Versailles, Antietam, Montgomery, Camelot, Bethlehem, Cambridge. The sound of your own name on somebody else's lips. Shouted down from a window, called out from a crowd of faces, the power that your name has to make you turn, to make you hear, to make you answer, to make you *be* your name. Yahweh telling Moses his name so that Moses could make God turn and be. Your own secret name written on a white stone and known only to you when at last you receive it. *Niemand weiss, niemand weiss/Dass Ich Rumpelstiltskin heiss*, and when the young queen is able at last to name her dwarfish tormentor, he is unable to torment her any longer and gives her back her heart again. The one who leads you to where you can name at last and face the faceless one who has stalked you for years through the thickets of your dreams.

The name of Jesus. Incarnation. All those years of waiting until finally the holy dream became a holy face. Like Sunday's face, perhaps, too frank to be understood, too obvious to be detected, his jokes so big and simple that no one had thought of them. The power beyond all powers which is the power to make Christs and Bodhisattvas, to make heroes out of pigs, to spin gold out of straw, that room at the heart of reality where life is born of death, it has a face, a name. Who would have guessed it?

He fell asleep in somebody's boat, and when the storm came up, they had to waken him. Looking down at the ground, he moved the dirt around with one finger, avoiding the face of the whore. At Cana there is wine on his breath as he speaks with chilling rudeness to his mother. On his ruined face, there is dried Roman spit. "Jesus, remember me when you come in your kingly power," the crook croaks to his left. "Remember me, remember me."

Peter said, "I have no silver and gold, but I give you what I have; in the name of Jesus of Nazareth, walk." And Peter took the cripple by the right hand, leathery and soft like a monkey's hand, and raised him up, and immediately his ankles and his feet were strong—not plump and pedicured feet like Prince Oblonsky's but withery little feet like hands that have been held under water too long. And all the people saw him walking, if you could call it walking, his arms jerking up and down and one knee twisted around almost backward, but walking anyway, praising God, and they recognized him as the one who sat for alms at the Beautiful Gate.

"In the name of Jesus of Nazareth," I say, that name at which every knee should bow in heaven and on earth and under the earth, "I bid that I fall into no sin this day nor run into any kind of danger." I do not pray. I exorcise. My concern is not now with the sin I commit, not now with all I do or fail to do that widens and darkens the space which you and I must reach across if we are ever to touch life into each other's lives. I do not now ask strength to resist the evil that I choose but invoke power to protect against the evil that chooses me for its alphabet. It is my game and I must believe also my calling in this high-ceilinged room to journey into myself, into the place where dreams come from, into the night, and not wishing to frighten anything away, I go there unarmed. Thus thoughts I do not choose to think choose me to think them. Cruelties, lusts, deceits, rise unbidden out of the shadows when I least expect them. Blasphemies gibber. Old grievances troop by in fantastic disguises. There is no tabloid horror, no crime or freak of flesh, which I cannot imagine becoming both my trick and my treat. Here in these inner places it is always Hallowe'en. They are a nice place to visit, but I wouldn't want to live there. The holy name of Jesus is my rabbit's foot, my charm against the evil eye and the dark.

And yet it is in this same dark that like Thursday I am commissioned. A face I cannot see, a voice that by faith alone I think I can recognize, says, "Come," says speak my true and lively word, says bring the good news into whatever bad news your feet may find, says translate such ragged glimpses of the mystery as you stumble on into F, G, H, I, J and into U, V, W. What's to be done? the plump Prince asks, staring down at those morocco slippers. Uncork your felt-tip. Write the date at the top of the page. For all I know, the whole creation holds its breath. The ant lays down its crumb and listens. I can think of a hundred places I would rather be. But this is my place.

On Michelangelo's ceiling, the old man reaches down out of the cloud to touch Adam's finger and give him life. Here the situation is reversed. I am Adam reaching up to touch an old man's finger and give life to a cloud. I am writing about an old man who exists only in my mind. I have put him together out of scraps and pieces, most of them forgotten. There's some of Mark Twain in him, the old Mark they brought back in a wheel chair from Bermuda to die at Stormfield. There's some of the old man Isak from Bergman's *Wild Strawberries* in him who at the end of the film looks across a little inlet and sees a young man and a young woman in Victorian dress

—the man in a straw hat fishing, the woman sitting on the grass beside him with a white parasol—and recognizing them as his parents, raises one hand in greeting as across the water one of them raises a hand to him. There's some of an old German cousin in him who looked like the Kaiser and walked through forests with his cane in the air naming trees. No need to list more of what went into my old man's making. It is enough to say that it is I who made him and not he himself. I speak not of Michelangelo's old man in the cloud but of the old man in the novel I am here to try to write. He is my old man, and it is in me that he lives and moves and has such being as he may be said to have.

It is true that he has never run away with the book as novelists are fond of saying their characters do, but he has on occasion lived and moved in ways other than those I had in mind for him. For instance, he weeps from time to time. I had imagined him as crustier and more remote than that. Also, although I intended him to see ghosts, I did not intend the particular ghosts that he saw—Elizabethan ghosts mainly. He saw Shakespeare's ghost whispering on and on with a faint lisp about forgotten rooms and forgotten faces, and he saw the ghost of Elizabeth herself. "She had the worst set of teeth I ever saw," my old man said, "as if she'd been eating blueberry pie. Now, the dress and all could have been a figment of my imagination," he went on. "The dress I could have dreamed, but not the teeth. It would have taken a dentist to dream a set of teeth like that." It was I obviously who put those words into the old man's mouth, but I had not planned on his saying them any more than the old man planned on the Queen's bad teeth. It is the same way, I suppose, as with people you dream about. They have only your dream to move around in and they are your creatures, but they move with a curious freedom. It is my godlike task this morning to start the old man moving again.

With the rain beginning to let up a little, I read back over the work of the last few days, an absurdly small amount for all the hours of my life I spent on it, only three or four pages in a script so nearly unreadable even to myself that I assume that at some level of my being I do not want it read, sentences written and rewritten and then so befuddled with interlineations that I have to copy them out all over again in order to read them and then in the process of copying rewrite them into illegibility again. I read it all over only to discover when I am finished that it is apparently not the words that I have been listening to but the silence in between the words maybe or the silence in this familiar room where I have spoken the name of Christ and signed myself with his cross. I have understood nothing of what I have read so I have to go back and read it all over again.

The old man whose name is Peter is on a journey with his two middle-aged sons and his grandson, and they stop in the woods to eat their lunch. The old man is the Tin Woodman who lacks a heart, one son is the Cowardly Lion who lacks courage, the other son is the Scarecrow who lacks a brain, and the grandson is the child who wants to go home but does not know where home is. Nowhere in the book are these parallels explicitly drawn, but knowing about them is helpful to me. The scene I read over again tells how, biting into his sandwich, the old man feels his eyes go suddenly hot and fill with tears. He feels stupid and ashamed because he doesn't know why he is weeping, but luckily the others do not notice. "He looked up at the crazy-quilt of leaves and noticed a ragged shape of air hanging down low enough for him to take hold of if he reached up. He would fold it back like the flap of a tent, and then they would see. Their mouths all milk and mayonnaise, their eyes dollying wide with wonder and astonishment, they would know that he had only to open it a fraction wider and they would be inundated, consumed, by the billowing flame." But he does not do this, just raises his arm and closes his fingers on the emptiness, then curls them up against the palms, chafing the whispering flesh, and lets his gaze sink slowly from the leaves to the scarecrow son biting the end off a pickle, the cowardly lion son shattered into fragments of light and dark. The scarecrow son has a gun with him, and for the madness of a moment the old man imagines that his son is going to shoot him with it, but this does not happen of course. Then comes a scene that I thought up before I thought up a book to put it in.

"See the big black flap-flap," the scarecrow says. He had crouched down lower, a bandy-legged squat with his rear end quivering as he adjusted his stance, the rifle raised to firing position. He was aiming back toward the road some fifty yards away where beneath the low-hanging tatter of leaves a large crow stood in the yellow dust. Like Sarah's coffee, bitter to the point of sourness, it was black to the point of blue-green, purple, as it fanned one wing out and strutted on clown's feet, a ragged, black rent in the road.

"Hushabah, hushabah, shoofly, scarecrow . . ." Tommy was doing his own little dance and whispering as he followed it with the wavering barrel of his gun until, collapsing the wing back in tight to its side, it turned to face him, and they both stood still—the dapper little funeral of a bird and Tommy with his flushed face caving in where the gunstock bit across one cheek. Only the Bermuda shorts trembled a little where they hung loose from his straining hams.

It was so quick and needle-sharp when it came that even before it has stopped whining in their ears, it was as if it had never happened, and silence came washing back in over them again, the canopy of leaves unstirring, the dusty grass a haze at the road's edge.

No squawk of flying feathers but slow and dark the

crow rose a few feet off the ground and came floating in under the trees on a lazy flip-flop of outspread wings like a boat with its oars feathered riding some green unhurried current. It made straight for Tommy through the low branches as though tracing back to its source the path that the bullet had blazed, drawing together again the raw new rift in the air. The flight seemed endless, a dream of flying, trance of wings, until abruptly then the end came and the bird fell like a rag at Tommy's feet. He got down on his knees and with both hands picked it up and touched it to his crumbling cheek. "Old croaker, old squawker," he said.[7]

It's a scene that doesn't do any of the things that I suppose scenes in novels are supposed to do, whatever else. It doesn't add to the characterization or advance the plot. But although it took me more hours to write than it is worth and although the sense of failure that I had when I finished it haunts me as I read it over again at my table now, I feel that something works in it, at least works for me. Something is trying at least to come to life in it, I decide, and glance up at Jane McWilliams' picture where something has come to life in those furious trees. What is the question Jesus answers?

Like old love letters, what I write usually makes me cringe with embarrassment when I reread it, but I like the crow scene at this moment and although what follows it I do not like so much, I decide that this morning

I will try to pick up something in the scene again and end the chapter with it. My heart beats like the heart of a man about to make a speech. This morning, I am sure, it will be different—not the laborious writing and rewriting with only a paragraph to show for three or four hours work, but instead here in the rain it will come spinning off my fingers as effortlessly as a letter to an old friend. Only to what friend am I writing, I wonder, and why do I write him this?

Then, as so often happens, just as I am ready to start writing, knowing pretty much what I want to say and excited about finding a way to say it well, something in me tries to get up and leave it—drink a glass of water, look out the window, read a magazine. Just as the spell has a chance of working, I break it. Just as there is a chance of bringing light out of dark, I choose the dark, withdraw my hand from the hand I have reached out for. If sleep is good for the sleeping children, does that mean that life is bad for them, bad for my old man and for me? If there is a will toward speaking and life, is there a will also toward silence and death so that each morning you have your choice whether to wake or not to wake? If there is a will to be known and forgiven, is there a will also to remain hidden? Yes, of course, but the full answer about why I both want to write and do not want to write lies deeper still, and were I to discover it, I would discover perhaps the secret name written on the white stone. I do not discover it. But this morning at least I resist the temptation to leave my work before I have begun it. For better or worse, I choose this time for life instead of death.

I want to bring the chapter back to the old man again. His scarecrow son, Tommy, has shot the crow and it has flown back to him and fallen at his feet. There is silence in the woods except that of course woods are never silent, only full of sounds that make them seem so. But the people are silent. Nobody speaks. One by one I try to see them there. The boy is lying on his stomach with his head craned around to watch his father, Tommy. The cowardly lion has his hand over his eyes for a visor. "What they had mistaken at first for silence," I write, "was the hushing and creak of the trees." For the moment that will have to do. But where is my old man, Peter? He is the one I need most to see. I try to dream him into the woods, to see his face, whether he is sitting down or standing. Adam, Adam, where art thou? Could anything be less important than the whereabouts of an imaginary old man in an imaginary wood, and yet my feet have taken me up the stairs to this room where his whereabouts are important. If anything is important, I must believe—for me, now—his whereabouts are important.

My eyes are fixed sightlessly on the window just beyond the writing table and remain fixed there for I have no idea how long. Finally their sight returns and I see that all this time I have been looking at the window without knowing that I was looking at it. Through it there is white picket fence across the street, and one of the blisters in the glass pane has taken an oval-shaped piece out of the fence and out of the grass beyond the fence; it looks as if there is some kind of hole in the world there, some kind of oval-shaped entrance to another world inside this world.

Where is my old man? It is just when I am not looking for him but looking at the window instead that I see him. He is sitting on one hip with his legs curled around in an awkward way and leaning on one arm with his hand pressed so hard to the earth that when he gets up, he will find the earth printed on his hand like a map. He is obviously thinking about this incident that he has witnessed, the crow hit and flying back, but I don't want to have him wonder out loud about what it means if anything. Does life have a plot? Maybe he is not thinking about the crow at all but just about how firm and unyielding the earth feels to the heel of his hand.

He seems extremely vulnerable to me at this moment. The air has lifted a wisp of his hair so that it looks as if somebody has cuffed him there. I forget to write that down for some reason. But it is his legs that tell me most about what is going on inside him, the queer way he has curled them up beside him. I see them very clearly. If I could manage to translate the look of those legs alphabetically, I would have translated much. I would have given the reader (who will read this and will his reading make any difference to him? I doubt it) something from which to translate back to the reality of the old man himself who is not quite real and to what is or is not going on inside him, inside me—his only begetter. I try five or six different translations, each time saying either too much or too little. Could anything matter less than how I say it? Could anything matter more?

Across the street there is a hole in the world, but it seems unlikely to make any difference to anybody. "Peter Ringkoping sat sideways under the tree leaning heavily on one arm," I write, "with his feet protruding at odd angles from his baggy pants." I had just *pants* but now I have *baggy pants*, an old man's pants that don't fit very well, a pair he bought a long time ago. Probably he had them pressed specially for this trip, but he has been riding in a car most of the day, perspiring, crossing and uncrossing his legs without pulling the creases out first, spilling things on them, and now they look like hell. Baggy. His feet stick out in the wrong places, turned the wrong way, almost as if they do not belong to him. The *lachrymae rerum*. The blister in the glass. Those enraged trees of Jane McWilliams' with the walrus crouched under them and whatever question it is that Jesus answers.

Then I think maybe I have it right about the legs at last. God knows how much time has gone by. The rain has stopped. I have made several unnecessary trips to the bathroom. But I know now how the old man's legs look.

They look broken. "Peter Ringkoping sat sideways under the tree leaning heavily on one arm with his feet protruding at odd angles from his baggy pants," I write, "as if his legs had been broken." His scarecrow son, that compulsive, middle-aged comedian in Bermuda shorts, has killed a bird, and now his eighty-year-old father sits there looking as though his legs have been broken.

Now will he know, I wonder, whoever reads this, if anybody does, picking it up maybe forty-five or fifty years from now in a second-hand book store or rummage sale—now will whoever reads this know what is going on inside the old man and outside too (he looks as though his legs have been broken) and will it make any difference to him to know it, whoever he turns out to be? O sweet Christ, does it make any difference to you with whose holy cross I have crossed myself? O Jane McWilliams, does it make any difference to you that his legs look broken? Is that why your trees are so mad?

For richer or poorer, for better or worse, in sickness and in health, I am a priest of Christ, knelt once in a circle of priests with all their flapjack hands heavy on my bald spot, and I have spent now Christ only knows how much of my unspeakably precious and grotesquely limited time on this holy day thinking up and then writing down B, R, O, K, E, N, that is how the old man's legs looked. O lamb of God which taketh away the sin of the world, have mercy upon us. Lord, have mercy upon us. *Kyrie eleison.* Was it truly your voice I heard in the pitch dark commissioning me to of all things this?

Beyond the blistered, wavy glass, there is the wet street of the world, the butcher's awning, the cat covering its mess. The world is in pain, and its pain makes strangers of us all and ties my tongue in a lover's knot. I remember the radio and the four year old whose parents punished him. You don't get water scalding all in a minute. You heat it on the stove or you let it run for awhile. They had to wait for this. They had to wait while the tub was filling. How far did they fill it? To his waist? To his shoulders? One of them had to get him out of bed. Was it the mother or the father, and did the other wait in the bathroom, or did they both go to get him together? Or did they have the child with them when they filled the tub? Did they take the child's pajamas off if he had any, or did they put him in naked? And which of them put him in? Scalding. Did they burn their hands or let him slide out of their hands, the hot, stringy child's arms forced straight up like the branches of Jane McWilliams' trees from the pressure of their hands as they let him slide into the tub?

The muffled, muddy deaths in Viet Nam. The ballooned out bellies of Biafran children. The stockpiling nations who with their mad prudence will risk peace for the sake of security but not security for the sake of peace. The poor people. "When Apollo II took off, I forgot all about the poor people for a few minutes,"

Ralph Abernathy said, or something like that, "but then I remembered them again"—the poor people of the world, the poor ones that he forgot and then remembered, the poor in wintertime and when it's raining, the poor breaking fast, breaking and fast, poor people's child climbing out of the Sunkist-colored bus in the rain. The black man and the white man. The black man sick and ashamed to be black, or proud to be black, or, like Elizabeth Bishop's boy who stood on the burning deck reciting "The boy stood on the burning deck," proud to be proud to be black. And the white man proud not to be proud to be white, or proud not to be black—the sadness of their battles and in both of their bloods, the sadness of the racial victory that is the human defeat, the sadness even of their truces sometimes, the black boy elected president of the class because he is black, the white boy and the black boy pretending they are the same when they are also in many comic and marvelous ways different and should be laughing and weeping and marveling at the marvelous differences between them.

I cannot easily enter into and feel and imagine the major pains that the world is dying of, but the pain of the child's punishment I càn imagine too easily. I cannot easily stop imagining it. By some queer and awful grace, I enter that screeching bathroom, basement, kitchen. I am the parents in their slapstick rage. I know the yammering that has kept them awake all night when night is their only wealth and peace. I know both the horror and the fascination of the torture. I am the scalded child, and I am also the water that scalds him. I am not Almighty God, but if I were, maybe I would in mercy either heal the unutterable pain of the world or in mercy kick the world to pieces in its pain.

Instead I sit in an empty Sunday-school room and write how a black crow rowed back through the air to fall like garbage at the feet of the clown who shot him and how the old man sits there in his baggy, old-man pants with his feet sticking out at odd angles as though his legs are broken.

The interlocutor speaks. He is sitting at the opposite end of the Harkness table where I teach, as if to raise the question which is the head of this table and which is the foot. He tips back his chair. "You mean you think you should be down there in the thick of it, right? Salving your conscience in one of the more plausible ghettos? Slogging it out beside Spock and Coffin. Marching on the Pentagon. Delivering turkeys at Christmastime. The trouble is you don't have the face for it, sir. You don't have either the face for it or the guts for it. If you ever left this room and entered the real war, you know what you'd end up doing, don't you?"

I know, of course, but I shake my head. I would rather have him be the one to say it.

"You'd end up rolling bandages," he says.

"Maybe I should be rolling bandages," I say.

Come unto me, all ye with guts and without guts, with

the right kind of face and the wrong kind of face. This is your first and last and only day. Be alive all day in it. Where your feet take you, that is who you are. My feet are crossed under the table where I write. The heel of one is pressed against the instep of the other. My legs are broken.

On the blackboard above her picture, Jane McWilliams has written *Jesus Answers a Question*. Through this story I am trying to write in this room about an old man's journey, I also want to answer a question. Perhaps it is the same question although I cannot be certain of this. My trouble is not only that I am not sure what the answer to my question is but that like Gertrude Stein on her deathbed, I am not even sure what the question is. I believe, however, that it has something to do with the price of being a human being. How much does a tin man have to pay for a heart? How much does a cowardly lion have to fork out for courage? What does it cost a scarecrow to be a man? Some question like that.

One day the old man in my book comes on a puddle of rainwater with the sky and the trees reflected in it. A bird is swimming there deeper than the tops of the deepest trees and there are fathoms and fathoms of sky still deeper than that. The old man has the impulse to jump down into this sky, but he resists the impulse. "When you are sick to your stomach and wish you were dead," he writes about it later, "there comes a moment

when you know that you must get the poison up somehow. But you do not stick your finger down your throat.
You swallow down the freshets of saliva that come
welling up into your mouth. You resist the protesting
spasms of your own bilge. Because the poison you have
to get rid of to be well is part of who you are, you will
not let it go without a rumpus. From my childhood, I
have never been able to retch without weeping. It was
the same at the edge of the puddle. I did not jump in
because I could not let myself go. Not even in order to
live could I let go my death."

Is the reason the trees are so angry that the walrus
is sick and refuses to vomit? Is it possible that it is not a
walrus at all but a crouching man and that what I took
for a large moustache is his mouth wide open because the
pain is more than he can handle with his mouth closed?
Is the question Jesus answers: "Good teacher, what
must I do to inherit eternal life?" and the answer when
all's said and done: "Come, follow me," which means—
following him—that one way or another you end up
with dried spit on your face if maybe only just your own
dried spit; means maybe that you end up with a sick
smile rolling bandages because some poor pig has to roll
them, or that you live with your guilt at not rolling
bandages but at doing instead whatever other crazy job
you like to think the voice in the dark room set you.

The man who was Thursday stood there in the dark.

"I really have no experience," he began.

"No one has any experience," said the other, "of Armageddon."

"But I am really unfit—"

"You are willing, that is enough," said the unknown.

"Well really," said Syme, "I don't know any profession of which mere willingness is the final test."

"I do," said the other. "Martyrs. I am condemning you to death. Good day." [8]

Maybe the creature under the tree has just been told that if he wants to live, first he has to die, and his mouth is wrenched open with what may be either a roar of great laughter or a wail of despair. What it costs to be a man, he is told, is everything he's got. To be rich, he must be willing to spend himself down to the last nickel. To be happy, he must be willing to let his heart break. To be blessed, he must be willing to live like a damned fool—giving not getting, losing not winning, reaching out into the night for a hand that's not there, dancing a dance that clack-clack is the only music to. The creature under the trees laughs very much like hell or cries like a banshee because of course this is all precisely and definitively what he can neither do nor be. He is not a man; he is a walrus. He is not a hero; he is a pig. His legs are broken.

I have chosen to wake up this morning rather than

not to wake up; I might have chosen otherwise. I have gladdened at the sight of rain. I have had my breakfast. I have said goodbye to my wife and children. In a town where there is grief and pain enough to turn the heart to stone, I have turned my back and climbed the thirteen stairs to this sheltering room. I have put a few labored and irrelevant words down on paper. A crow gets shot. If there is in heaven or on earth or under the earth anywhere any justification for my presence at this table in this room it is that I have something so good to say that I can be forgiven everything else if I will only say it. I must believe that I have such a thing to say. I do not always believe it. Let somebody else now say it for me.

Let Louis Armstrong say it. Why not? Maybe that is Satchmo under Jane McWilliams' trees saying it now, singing it out with his mouth wide open. It is an old Gospel hymn that New Orleans bands used to play when a lodge member died, marching down the pike to the graveyard. First there is just the solo boom of the bass drum dead-march slow—four big, hollow booms, two longs and two shorts, so deep and heavy that like Arlo's organ you can feel them in your teeth. Then very slow and a little sour the band comes in all loose and rattly like something being pulled along by mules. Then a horn takes it, fogged up and lonesome at first and then gradually, though still very slow, getting almost too hot to touch. Then Louis starts to sing. The black face tipped up to the sweaty kliegs. The yellow eyeballs bugging out. The rubber lips shaking all around that crazy hallelujah of teeth. The s's hissing like cotton-mouths. The tortured, orgasmic grin.

"Just—a closer walk—with Thee,

O Lord—grant it, if you please," with the big drum boom-booming and the lazy chicken-hawk spirals of the hot horn.

> *"I am weak but—Thou art strong.*
> *O Lord—keep me from all wrong.*
> *I'll be satisfied as long*
> *As I walk—let me walk—close to Thee."*

You are weak, but he is strong. You are a pig, but he is a hero. Your legs are broken, but his are not, not a bone in his body is broken. But he so loved. The world. So loved it. The alphabet of his grace is sufficient. His jokes are so big and simple no one has thought of them. Walk close.

Go tell it on the mountain. Go tell it to the Marines. Just maybe it is true. It may just maybe be that it is as they have always said it was. It is not you who have created the old man but the old man who created you. Simeon Stylites on his stilt; Billy Sunday rigged out like a traffic cop; the holy martyrs up to their crotches in fire; Tillich, Calvin, Dante, at their electric typewriters; Michelangelo crawling like a spider across his ceiling; Bach with his fingers in the air—good ones and bad ones, fat ones and thin ones, stupid ones and clever ones, ugly and beautiful ones, some with their feet on the ground and some as queer as Dick's hatband. It may just be that it is maybe as they have all of them always said it was, I suppose only half believing it most of the time, never by a long bloody shot having quite received it, but seeing it and greeting it from afar. And telling it. Telling it to the Marines. Telling it on the mountain. If only *maybe* it is true—may be—the *maybe* alone is maybe of all things most worth telling, even if clumsily through an alphabet of old men and dead crows: the gladdest, wildest, goodest, gravest and gayest thing there anywhere is to tell. That the secret of the universe is a room where life is reborn out of death. A room where you are commissioned in darkness. A room where the white wicker rocker ticks and morning after morning you are given back the world. A room in a dream where you write out a name in the wet. This room where you are now, crowded with angels.

Or maybe the way they have told it is only a metaphor for the way it truly is. And since to tell it the way it truly is beggars all alphabets, maybe the wilder the metaphor the nearer the wildness of truth. Maybe it is time to *re*mythologize this gorgeous Gospel. The spelling out of grace can never be phonetic. It can only approximate the true sounds. The alphabet is finally the Hebrew alphabet. There are nothing but consonants, and it is left to the faithful to fill in the vowels with faith.

It is time for lunch, and with infinite relief I put the pen in my pocket, the ABC notebook in my briefcase. I put on my raincoat although it has stopped raining. It is time to say goodbye to Jane McWilliams, but I leave without remembering to say it. Any day now they may erase Jane McWilliams. We are none of us safe and may none of us be remembered.

The air is cool and gray, and it is absurdly good to be out in it again. I am a child let out of school by a snow-storm. I am waking up in my own bed to discover that the wicked witch was only a dream and the lion just Bert Lahr dressed up. I am being told that the x-rays turned out after all to be perfectly normal. I am the Man in the Iron Mask getting a shave. The wet pavement rings like New Year's Eve under my feet, and the thought of lunch comes down out of heaven like a bride adorned for her husband. It is no longer my first and last and only day. I have lived already close to fifteen thousand days, and with luck I may live fifteen thousand more. Even at seventy-five cents extra, I may have the shrimp cocktail.

I am to meet a friend for lunch, but I am early. It is a small, dark lobby that smells of raincoats even when it is not raining, and I sit near the revolving rack of picture postcards. The woman at the desk has a bell the shape of a birthday cake. The slight ache in my arm is only be-cause I must have slept on it wrong, and it is a good ache, the kind that reminds you you are alive.

I wait for my friend, and, waiting, I am neither this

nor that but in between somewhere, and it is on my friend that what I become next depends. Unlike me, he is a real priest, a priest with a parish who also dresses like a priest, and we are likely to be nervous and over-excited in each other's presence. Half the time neither of us is quite sure what the other is talking about, which is partly because we both talk too fast about too many things and partly because we do not so much listen, I think, as in our eagerness listen to ourselves listen. But sometimes a hand waves back across the inlet of air between us. If it does, I will become one thing. If it does not, I will become another. And he too, I suppose. We are in each other's hands. I must remember to ask him if he knows who Jane McWilliams is.

It is of course the Messiah I am waiting for. The door is always left open for him and an extra place set at the table. One by one the Central Council of the anarchists drop their fantastic disguises and turn out to be police-men. Dr. Bull takes off his terrifying black spectacles, and the man who was Thursday discovers beneath them a very boyish-looking young man with frank and happy hazel eyes wearing cockney clothes like those of a city clerk. The smile is still there, but it no longer freezes the blood; it might be the first smile of a baby as he slaps down the official blue card that he also received in the dark room. Who knows in what partial way the long expected one appears, in what disguise the one who is to come comes.

I was riding down the mountain once in a red pick-up truck with a friend who is built like Popeye, all barrel chest and pasture-prowling legs. He has one bad eye, but the profile I am looking at is the one with the good eye, and I watch it as he talks. He talks about the weather: thunder in the fall, no winter at all, and my God, he says, when a man gets to be almost sixty, he's not what he once was. The rattlesome cab of the truck stutters like a confessional. It is his profile I watch. The socket of his eye. The bridge of his nose curves up to become the jut of his brow making a ruined Piranesi arch, the baths of Caracalla, the Palais des Papes where shadows hang like fishermen's nets from the vaulted roof, the cool, powdery scent of the stone. It is Saul in his cave keeping watch for David. It is stout Cortez upon a peak in Darien. The road which is all roads stretches out from his journeying eye. He is a small man in a vast and vaulted place. It is the heavenly council, and all the sons of God have gathered to present themselves before the Lord. The great Buddhas of the Prajna Paramita sutras are there trying to trick each other into making false distinctions between god and no-god, Nirvana and Samsara.

The disciple Subhuti said: "Profound, O Venerable One, is the perfect Transcendental Wisdom."

Quoth the Venerable One: "Abysmally profound,

like the space of the universe, O Subhuti, is the perfect Transcendental Wisdom."

The disciple Subhuti said again: "Difficult to be attained through Awakening is the perfect Transcendental Wisdom, O Venerable One."

Quoth the Venerable One: "That is the reason, O Subhuti, why no one ever attained it through Awakening." [9]

And then one may imagine, Heinrich Zimmer says, that they burst together into peals of cosmic laughter.

The Baalim are there and also "mooned Ashtaroth . . . the Tyrian maids their wounded Thamuz mourn . . . and sullen Moloch . . . the brutish gods of Nile . . . Isis and Orus and the dog Anubis." [10] Square and short in his Big Jim coveralls, Popeye is called forth. He has been summoned to speak for mankind because he is an honest man, honest even when nobody ·is looking, honest even when you take him by surprise. He sits there behind the wheel squinting up at the gray sky, worried and quiet and eagle-eyed. He is at this moment in time our only mediator and advocate.

I am no longer early for lunch. My friend is late. They have laid down a path of green rubber that runs from the main entrance to the reservation desk. If you squinny a little, it looks like grass and you can imagine that spring has come to this lobby. The woman at the desk pats down twice on the birthday cake, and out of a leatherette armchair in the corner a seventy-year-old bell boy pulls himself up.

And behold, a virgin shall conceive and bear a son and shall call his name . . . God knows what. I will pretend that I have forgotten his name, but admit to remembering his face. It is a bony, handsome, sand-colored face. He is a minister, and I am studying to become one. We meet in his office at Riverside Church to discuss the possibility of my doing some kind of part-time work there. He looks grave and tired as he outlines what there might be for me. Years before in another world I had known him slightly, or at least knew who he was. We went to the same college, and at football games he would rise up in the stands after successful plays and give a red-hot jazzy blast on his trumpet like the angel of the resurrection. Sometimes he dressed up to look like a tiger and entertained the fans during rest periods, or maybe that was somebody else. I no longer remember what I was dressed up to look like.

There is a great deal of pastoral calling to be done, he tells me now—families of blacks, whites, Puerto Ricans to touch, just the hem of their garments. There is also an opening in Christian Education—someone to stand up at a lectern and make speeches. I say that maybe I could handle this. It is where my experience has been. I don't think I would be too good at the calling. There are shadows under his eyes, and he clasps his hands behind his head. "You like to be in the limelight," he says. And out of his mouth issues a sharp two-edged sword, and his face is like the sun shining in full strength.

He has named my name. The limelight. Why else am I here at this lectern now rather than off at some Christlier task, rolling bandages if that's the best I can do. Why not? Am I so in love with the sound of my own voice and with the feeling of many eyes upon me? Am I here to make myself believe that I am better than my face? Am I here to make myself believe that I will never die? It is my moment in the sun, my chance to be known and forgiven. It is a chance to put my thumb on your hearts. Less for Christ's sake, then, than for my own sake maybe am I here at this lectern in this light? The pig's curly tail pokes out from beneath the black Geneva gown.

Sweet Christ, forgive and mend me. Forgive me the limelight which to love is my sin, which to gaze into is to go blind. Yet if I desire the limelight, I also dread it. Because it burns as it illumines. Because it is the invisible spotlight that moves from life to life in the New Hampshire basement where questions are asked and judgments made. It is the gaudy spot now amber, now crimson, but finally bright as moonshine that shows up the spots on Arlo's rented tuxedo and illumines the difference between what is maybe true and what it surely schmaltz. It is the hot kliegs that send the sweat like tears down Satchmo's face. So if it is my sin, it is also my salvation. Where sin abounds, grace abounds all the more. In the limelight I catch a mercifully unmerciful glimpse of myself. Come, thou long awaited one, redeemer and judge, with healing in thy wings.

The woman at the desk calls out my name. She mispronounces it. Maybe with the lectern and the limelight what I want more than anything else is simply for people to know how to pronounce my name. Maybe, as Dostoyevski said about old Karamazov, "even the wicked are much more naive and simple-hearted than we suppose. And we ourselves are too." I could always change the spelling of my name to be phonetic, but then it would no longer be my name. The umlauts of the fathers are visited upon the heads of the sons. My name is mispronounced, but it is my name, it is me, and I rise from my seat at the sound of it. The message that the woman gives me is that someone has called to say that my friend cannot make it for lunch. The one I have been waiting for is not going to come, and I am Estragon waiting for Godot, I am the old man in the woods reaching up to a shape of air and closing his fingers down on emptiness. But in many disguises he has come before, and in many disguises he will come again before he comes finally, and once or twice I have even thought I recognized him. I watch the waiter suspiciously as I eat my lunch alone. I decide against the shrimp cocktail.

And what more shall I say? For time would fail me to tell of Gideon, Barak, Samson, Jephthah, of David and

Samuel and the prophets. All these also did not receive
what was promised but greeted it from afar, and then
there are all those who did not much believe in the
promise to begin with, and it is not always possible to
tell the two apart. The man burning leaves by the side
of the road as I drive home. The woman who had to
have all her teeth pulled at once and whose face is so
changed that I cannot help believing that she is herself
changed because she was her face and now it is another
face. The man at the post office who when I ask him how
he likes being retired says that he likes it all right but
misses the vacations. Do they believe that at the heart
of the universe there is a room? Or do they believe that
there is no heart to the universe, just down, down, and
that the dark crow that rows back through the air marks
us all for its own and darkness's? I do not know what
they believe. They would never say unless I pressed
them, maybe not even then, and I would never press
them. The most crucial thing is always the thing that is
not said. They are simply getting on with their lives,
and it is not so simple. Maybe that is the most crucial
thing.

"I hear you are entering the ministry," the woman
said down the long table, meaning no real harm. "Was
it your own idea or were you poorly advised?" And the
answer that she could not have heard even if I had given
it was that it was not an idea at all, neither my own nor
anyone else's. It was a lump in the throat. It was an itch-

ing in the feet. It was a stirring in the blood at the sound of rain. It was a sickening of the heart at the sight of misery. It was a clamoring of ghosts. It was a name which, when I wrote it out in a dream, I knew was a name worth dying for even if I was not brave enough to do the dying myself and could not even name the name for sure. Come unto me, all ye who labor and are heavy laden, and I will give you a high and driving peace. I will condemn you to death.

I pick the children up at the bottom of the mountain where the orange bus lets them off in the wind. They run for the car like leaves blowing. Not for keeps, to be sure, but at least for the time being, the world has given them back again, and whatever the world chooses to do later on, it can never so much as lay a hand on the having-beenness of this time. The past is inviolate. We are none of us safe, but everything that has happened is safe. In all the vast and empty reaches of the universe it can never be otherwise than that when the orange bus stopped with its red lights blinking, these two children were on it. Their noses were running. One of them dropped a sweater. I drove them home.

And what more shall I say? For time would fail me to tell of how the dead leaves lie in drifts around the front door, of how this particular house smells when you come into it out of a gray and lonesome October after-

noon. Time would fail me to tell of how it annoys me
that my wife hasn't bothered to get the morning's mail
out of the mailbox yet and how it annoys her when I tell
her so, and how in secret we both enjoy the annoyance
which is solid and real and reminds us that our lives are
wondrously linked.

Huntley and Brinkley are depressing although the
news has nothing badder in it than usual, but rum and
cider help. Supper is late and Wagnerian. The dirty
dishes are endless. Eating is endless, three times a day,
year after year. If they piled up all the food you have
ever eaten in one pile, how big a pile would it be? If they
added up all the hours you have spent sleeping, how
many hours, how many years, would you turn out to
have slept? Time would fail me. Time will fail us all, and
Gideon and Barak, Samson and Jephthah too. Getting
the children to bed is wild and complex, and not long
afterward we go to bed ourselves. Over the mantle,
Winslow Homer's croquet players wait by their wickets
in the dark.

Sleep is a threshold I drift toward like leaves. Brown
and sere as a leaf, a face drifts toward me, the eyes
buzzard-amber and burning. Is it true, my dear dead
dear? Is all of it true? Is any of it true? If there's anywhere to be now, you must be there. If there's anything
to know now wherever you are, then you must know it.
But I can dream no sure and certain answer onto the old

lips, just the faintest inclination of the black-felt tricorne. The face becomes a map of the world, becomes
the world itself seen from a great height.

An alphabet tumbles slowly like leaves sinking in deep
water. A is a tent with the flap pinned back and a bar
across. B is binoculars to bring the far a little nearer. C
is a crescent moon to see by. D, E, F, and G and H fall
and turn like dreams. I, J, K and L, M, N float lazily
down through the dark. It is a pool in the woods, and
O, P and Q and R and S are the carp, mud-slow and
glinting. Then T, then U, waving like weeds from the
bottom. V, W, X, and Y. Z darts by like an arrow.
Alphabet. Alpha, beta. Alpha, omega. Aleph, tau.

Half drowned in my pillow, a sleepy, shiftless prayer
at the end. Rejoice in the Lord always; again I will say,
Rejoice. O Thou. Thou who didst call us this morning
out of sleep and death. I come, we all of us come, down
through the litter and the letters of the day. On broken
legs. Sweet Christ, forgive and mend. Of thy finally un-
speakable grace, grant to each in his own dark room
valor and an unnatural virtue. Amen.

AUTHOR'S NOTES

1. FREDERICK BUECHNER, *The Final Beast* (New York: Atheneum, 1965; San Francisco: Harper & Row, 1982, pp. 175-178, *passim.*

2. LEO TOLSTOY, *Anna Karenina* (New York: Modern Library), p. 6.

3. MARK TWAIN, *Extract from Captain Stormfield's Visit to Heaven* (New York: Harpers, 1909), pp. 19–20.

4. MARK TWAIN, *The Mysterious Stranger* (New York: Harpers, 1916), p. 151.

5. G. K. CHESTERTON, *The Man Who Was Thursday* (New York: Dodd, Mead, 1923), pp. 233–234, 272–274, *passim.*

6. FREDERICK BUECHNER, *The Final Beast*, pp. 180–182, *passim*.

7. FREDERICK BUECHNER, *The Entrance to Porlock* (New York: Atheneum, 1970), pp. 134–135. Copyright © 1969 by the author. Used by permission of the publisher.

8. G. K. CHESTERTON, *The Man Who Was Thursday*, pp. 63–64.

9. Quoted by HEINRICH ZIMMER in *Philosophies of India* (New York: World, 1957; a Meridian Book), p. 487.

10. JOHN MILTON, "On the Morning of Christ's Nativity."